OVERWHELMED
BY THE
SPIRIT

This Book
Belongs To

Sally Hogan

DESTINY IMAGE BOOKS BY JAMES MALONEY

The Panoramic Seer

OVERWHELMED
BY THE
SPIRIT

EMPOWERED TO MANIFEST THE GLORY OF GOD
THROUGHOUT THE EARTH

JAMES MALONEY

DESTINY IMAGE® PUBLISHERS, INC.
P.O. Box 310, Shippensburg, PA 17257-0310
"Promoting Inspired Lives."

This book and all other Destiny Image, Revival Press, MercyPlace, Fresh Bread, Destiny Image Fiction, and Treasure House books are available at Christian bookstores and distributors worldwide.

For a U.S. bookstore nearest you, call 1-800-722-6774.
For more information on foreign distributors, call 717-532-3040.
Reach us on the Internet: www.destinyimage.com.

ISBN 13 TP: 978-0-7684-0357-2
ISBN 13 Ebook: 978-0-7684-8487-8

For Worldwide Distribution, Printed in the U.S.A.
2 3 4 5 6 7 8 / 17 16 15 14

To Mario Murillo.

CONTENTS

1

CREATOR

A FEW NIGHTS BACK, THE LORD JESUS CAME TO ME.

Probably right now warning sirens are going off in your brain, and you're wise to be a little cautious. When people say God appeared to them, you should be wary; not critical, just careful. But for those of you who've read my previous books (Thanks!), I trust you know by now I don't make statements like that flippantly. I know I'll stand before God to give an account to their accuracy, and I have a reverential fear of the Lord, so I dare not embellish or make up encounters such as this.

So, the Lord *did* appear to me. I saw Him as the Son of Man, dressed simply in a white robe and sandals, with medium-length brown hair, of average height and build, of Jewish descent. He wasn't serious, nor was He frivolous. His demeanor was very matter of fact, like what He was about to show me just *was*. *This is the way things are.*

I have spent the past few days in prayer, trying to process exactly how to share this encounter with you. I even submitted it to other prophets, asking if they received a confirmation. It's difficult, because I believe I was bodily *with* the Lord. Yes, it was night-time, but I wasn't simply dreaming this, and it didn't seem like a trancelike vision. While I cannot say unequivocally I was translated or transported with Him, I am firmly persuaded that is the case; similar to Paul not knowing whether he was in the body or out, as he wrote about in Second Corinthians 12.

Also, this experience was in real time. I mean, it didn't skip around like a dream: an hour was an hour. When I came to myself, sitting on my bed, I was dirty with dust, as if I'd just traveled through an arid area, and I had to get up and take a shower. I was exhausted and perspiring as if I'd participated in a three-hour miracle service. And that's just what happened.

It was as if I saw a map showing Uzbekistan, Kazakhstan, and Kyrgyzstan, countries that are located north and east of Iran and Afghanistan. This was a region, an area of operation that I saw. I can describe the terrain: dry and hilly with scrubby plants, not barren desert, but still rather dusty and semiarid. It was *hot*, early afternoon, which would make sense considering the time difference from Texas where I live.

The Lord impressed upon me that we were here because the people we were going to minister to had received the message of salvation from a missionary who had previously labored in this region. The plan of salvation had been preached, but the full gospel had not been presented with the Lord's miraculous touch following, proving the validity of what the missionary shared; so the people still labored horribly under the yoke of oppression. *He* had come to show them salvation was for *this* time, not just when they passed away. *He* had come to show them He was the God of miracles—in this life and the next.

I followed Jesus as He walked through the center of this area. I could see Him as if I were seeing you; He was not an apparition, nor was He in my "mind's eye." This was not a movie; I was beside Him. My senses were heightened as He turned to the left or to the right, and suddenly I noticed the people.

Picture, if you will, every kind of conceivable sickness, infirmity, disease, corruption, deformity, crippling condition known to humankind. Every cancer you've ever heard of, every malformed limb you've ever seen. Leprosy, genetic abnormalities, dwarfism, AIDS, crooked, withered arms and legs, amputations, polio, mental retardation, bloated, twisted bodies. They were all here in this region. I had never seen such a sea of human suffering and disease, and I've been to some pretty awful places on this earth!

I ached for these poor souls' plight; my stomach wrenched with compassion for them. Was Jesus going to heal?

Yes. Of course He was! Why else had He come?

He turned to the left or to the right as we walked slowly, and we beheld a man, if you could call him that, emaciated and contorted, drawn up legs and mangled arms, lying at the Lord's feet. He was about three feet tall and weighed maybe sixty pounds. His stomach was bloated, his ribs were protruding. There was no sign of humanity in his eyes, no cognizance or recognition. He was a vegetable.

Here's where you need to pay attention, because you'll miss the whole point of this testimony. As the man came into focus, at our Lord's feet, I was now seeing through Jesus' eyes, as if the man was laying at *my* feet. And now as I reached out my hands, I recognized them as my own, but they were the Lord's hands—as if He'd stepped into me and was moving through me. Or I had stepped into Him.

I want to point out, this had nothing to do with something coming from myself at all. The power was totally the Lord's alone, but He was choosing to move through me. I was completely surrendered to His will. Where He moved, I moved. My hands were His hands, His hands were my hands. My legs were His legs, His legs were my legs.

These Bible verses came to me:

> *Beware lest anyone cheat you through philosophy and empty deceit, according to the tradition of men, according to the basic principles of the world, and not according to Christ.* **For in Him dwells all the fullness of the Godhead bodily; and you are complete in Him, who is the head of all principality and power** (Colossians 2:8-10).

> *For we are members of His body, of His flesh and of His bones* (Ephesians 5:30).

> *For in Him we live and move and have our being, as also some of your own poets have said, "For we are also His offspring"* (Acts 17:28).

I understood what these passages meant: we are complete through our union in Christ, given His fullness as He is the head of all authority. I was no longer *just* myself, I was *in* Christ and He in me.

> *And of His fullness we have all received, and* **grace for grace** (John 1:16).

Grace for grace. This experience was a progression. This went beyond panorama, or prophetic utterance, speaking the word of the Lord. It went beyond moving in the gifts of the Spirit, as vitally important as that is. This went beyond operating in the level of personal or ministerial anointing that Christ gave as a measure to humankind (see Eph. 4:7). This wasn't just allowing the anointing to flow through me. This was turning myself over to the anointing of His life and being consumed by it. This was the physical, bodily representation of *all* He stood for, all of His power and might, moving through an empty, earthen vessel, because He *wanted* to operate this way.

It wasn't me (and yet it was) but rather it was Christ *in* me, the hope of glory (see Col. 1:27) I was utterly consumed by His fullness.

I realized what it meant to manifest the sonship of God, to be *His* and allow Him free reign to move as He, the God of all, saw fit. In almost half a century of salvation, almost forty years of ministry in the miraculous, this was, without question, *the single most profound experience of my life,* apart from getting saved. I cannot impress upon you enough just how radical this experience was. I can only pray the Spirit downloads some measure of revelation of what I'm trying to express here feebly.

I laid my/His hands on the wasted, vegetative man. There was no struggle, there was no fight against the demonic. There was no binding, loosing, praying, sobbing, begging, spitting or sputtering. The man was healed. It's as simple as that.

Within ten seconds, he was standing before me/Him, the proper weight, the proper height, all infirmity and lameness gone, his eyes were clear, and he praised God in his native tongue. He'd grown nearly three feet in less than a quarter of a minute.

Before I could even comprehend what I was seeing, I was now watching the Lord walk ahead of me again. He turned to another person, a child with a crippling condition; his limbs were withered. Once again, I found myself in Jesus, or Him in me, and as I stretched forth my/His hand toward the child, before I even knew what to say, he was whole, scampering on perfectly formed legs.

The next person Jesus stooped to pray for was actually two people, conjoined twins. As I beheld them through my/Jesus' eyes, they separated into two whole people instantly. I think we had barely laid hands on them.

A clamor arose as the two people, who were once joined, twirled in joy. Other people started appearing in this area we were standing in. Dozens, hundreds. They started bringing the sick before the Lord and laying them at His feet, begging for just a touch of His creative power to flow through them.

The verse that is to be the text for this whole book (so memorize it, please) appeared before me:

> *And Jesus went about all Galilee, teaching in their synagogues, preaching the gospel of the kingdom, and healing all kinds of sickness and all kinds of disease among the people. **Then His fame went throughout all Syria**; and they brought to Him all sick people who were afflicted with various diseases and torments, and those who were demon-possessed, epileptics, and paralytics; and He healed them* (Matthew 4:23-24).

Fame. What does that mean, really? Renown, yes. Recognition, yes. Eminence, prominence, notoriety, distinction, illustriousness. Reputation, yes! That's what we'll discuss throughout the course of this book, biblical concepts about God's fame. See, just as Jesus spread the fame of the Father's authority and power, I believe we—*through the aggressive, invasive, overwhelming help of the Holy Spirit, the glorious Intruder*—are to spread the fame of Jesus near and far. How do we do this? Well, hang in there—you've got about another 40,000 words to go, give or take; but first let's talk about the Man Jesus Christ who is God.

JESUS, THE SON OF MAN

We must recognize that Jesus' favorite term for Himself was "Son of Man," emphasizing His complete humanity. We know that Philippians 2:7 speaks of Christ emptying Himself, taking on the form of a servant, coming as a Man. On this earth He was totally reliant upon the Holy Spirit to move supernaturally. Otherwise we could have no hope of following in His footsteps if He operated in the miraculous as God only.

While on the earth, Jesus was not omniscient, omnipotent, nor omnipresent. He was limited as humankind is, needing the help of the Holy Spirit, the enabling of the anointing to perform the deeds recorded in the Gospels.

When Jesus told Nathanael He saw him under the fig tree (see John 1:48), that wasn't because Jesus was operating as God and knew everything. He relied upon a word of knowledge from the Holy Spirit.

The Lord chose to empty Himself of all rights and privileges to operate as deity, limiting Himself while on earth, to move only as the Father dictated through the Spirit. Jesus set aside His sovereignty, His total dominion over anything in creation. This emptying of Christ's authority to operate as God is called *kenosis* in the Greek.

However, Jesus did *not* stop being God (see John 3:13; 8:23; 8:58); He did not set aside His deity, for He was fully God and fully Man on the earth. However, He did set aside His divine rights to move as God. This is why He favored calling Himself the Son of Man, completely Man, reliant upon God the Spirit to move in a supernatural way.

It's a fine line to walk, not overemphasizing Jesus' divinity at the expense of His humanity, and vice versa. I believe Gordon Lindsay had a phenomenal way of explaining the "emptying" of Christ's godly authority, so that we may follow His example of being anointed by the Spirit, without sacrificing the just-as-vital truth of recognizing that Jesus was and is still God. I have attempted to outline it briefly, but I'm sure I've not done it as well as he did. In a future series called *Aletheia Eleutheroo*, I will dedicate more time to the *kenosis*.

It is true: while on this earth, Jesus was filled with the Holy Spirit, anointed by an all-encompassing Helper who was more than just a tagalong. Our Lord set the example for us to follow. I find that for the most part, we are simply imitating Him—and that's important, don't misunderstand (see Eph. 5:1). I'm not downplaying the moves of the Spirit that we have experienced by operating as imitators of

Christ. But I am convinced—especially after this encounter with the Lord—that there is a deeper level of ministry, with the help of the Spirit, that goes beyond just *imitating*, as key as that is.

Rather, in these latter days, we are to *manifest* the Lord Himself, give expression to His very nature through us! I believe the *ultimate* of ministry expression will come in these end times as a group of people catch hold of this concept and manifest the Lord in a way we've not seen much of in the past.

I think this ties into the Dove Company Frances Metcalfe spoke about in her eschatological visions: a forthcoming sonship genera- tion being preceded by a group of forerunners—I think we are the start of this manifestation. It's not *just* being a joint-heir with the Son, imitating His earthly actions (and yes, this is a true, right notion); but further, it is the sons of God being so emptied of self, that Christ *the* Son manifests through them. The sons liter- ally manifest *the* Son. The word *literal* means "actually, in actuality, really, truly."

That's what it means in Romans 8. All of creation is travailing, waiting for something. What? The revealing of the sons of God— through the help of the Holy Spirit aggressively tearing down our weaknesses (flesh). The whole planet eagerly awaits the thousands of earthen vessels of clay to manifest the Son of God as sons of God.

In other words, to the people, we become as the Son of God in man- ifestation. Of course, it's His life shining within us and through us.

A SON AND THE SON

But see the difference between imitating Christ as a son of God and manifesting Christ as *the* Son? It is a deeper progression. Yes, I believe the Son of God will manifest Himself through thousands of people in this end-time ministry. (Read *Ladies of Gold* for more information, if you're so inclined.) I pray this book will be a catalyst and a forerunner for the Dove Company.

Caution: I'm talking about a decrease of self here, not a cause for pride as in, "Jesus is manifesting Himself through me! Check it out!" (Again, for balance, read *The Panoramic Seer* on brokenness and humility—the two most vital elements of this manifestation.) *"He must become greater; I must become less"* (John 3:30 NIV). It is inversely proportional: the more He manifests through us, the less there is of *us*. It has to be that way because the anointing will not be poured out on unsanctified flesh (see Exod. 30:32); and let's face it, friend, we're a bunch of flesh! So before you start thinking that Dr. Maloney is spouting some kind of demigod garbage—check your ego at the door, please.

I think sometimes we've placed a whammy on ourselves when we minister to people. Like we've got to be *just* like Jesus, we have to be just as anointed as He was. And while there is a principle to this notion (I've written books about it!), let us never forget that Jesus is still fully God while He remains fully Man. There are operations that He does through us that we cannot hope to attain apart from allowing His divinity to shine through. Don't forget that even on the earth, the Lord was given the Spirit *without measure,* according to John the Baptist (see John 3:34). And he would know—Jesus called him the greatest prophet (see Matt. 11:11).

Yes, we imitate Him, relying upon the Spirit to anoint us in a measure. But I am just as equally convinced that in these latter days, forerunners are going to spring up who, through the help of the same Spirit, will become living conduits for Christ's ascension authority to pour through them. I believe when the end comes, whenever that is, there will be thousands of these Dove Company members.

So yes, while on the earth, Jesus ministered as a Man full of the Holy Spirit. But Christ has ascended, He has been glorified. He has returned to His full status in authority and dominion as the God of all. He not only encompasses what it means to be fully Man, but now, seated at the right hand of the Father, all of His ability and sovereignty to act as God has been restored. He is moving in us as fully God and fully Man. We cannot overstress one truth at the expense of the other.

There is an element of Christ's work through us that we can never hope to touch, nor should we! *We are not just supposed to be doing things the* same *as Jesus, because it is supposed to be Jesus doing it* through *us.* It's not us doing anything, but Christ *in* us. The revelation He gave me in this experience was liberating and revolutionary. We need to die to the flesh-mind, flesh-body, flesh-soul in order to be more hidden in Christ so it is Him who manifests through us as fully God! The greater works He spoke about (see John 14:12) are really just *His* works on a mass scale through His Body as He is manifesting His fully Godness (made up word) through us, based on His ascension and glorification.

> *I have been crucified with Christ;* **it is no longer I who live, but Christ lives in me**; *and the life which I now live in the flesh I live by faith in the Son of God, who loved me and gave Himself for me* (Galatians 2:20).

Thank God we have a revelation of Christ's humanity and how we are to imitate His operation as a human! But *in* Christ, I think there is a revelation of His divinity moving through us that the Spirit is bringing about in these latter days. He was still God on this earth, anointed by the Dove; He is still God now, glorified and ascended; and He expects to manifest that way as **God** through His people.

It isn't *only* us trying to move like Him in imitation, *"For you died, and your life is hidden with Christ in God"* (Col. 3:3). We're "dead," remember? Rather, we must set aside *ourselves* in the flesh so Christ, within us, can work out through us. We must become dead to the flesh, the soul, the mind, the body. Our only life is *in* Christ, hidden away, so He shows forth as God through us. That is the hope of glory! Glory, the weightiness, the reputation, the *fame* of God echoing to every corner of creation.

Jesus' relationship to the Father echoes the same revelation of ourselves being hidden in the Lord. It is a progression: the Son in the Father, us in the Son—and all of this through the help of a *forceful, assertive, insistent, uncompromising, and hard-hitting* glorious Intruder: the Holy Spirit crashing through our lives.

> *Do you not believe that I am in the Father, and the Father in Me? …Believe Me that I am in the Father and the Father in Me, or else believe Me for the sake of the works themselves. …At that day you will know that I am in My Father, and you in Me, and I in you. …He who has seen Me has seen the Father* (John 14:10-11,20,9).

I want you to note that all of this "Father in Me, Me in you" revelation from the Lord is in the context of the Holy Spirit being released to His children.

✳✳✳

People were arranged before us on bedrolls. Some didn't even show vital signs. One person had no arms, no legs, just a torso. Jesus veered into the crowds, and again I was inside Him, or vice versa, however it can be described. Then a person just unfolded, like a rose, and leapt onto instantaneously formed limbs. I'm talking *these* kinds of miracles.

The Lord just walked among the people, not flamboyantly or jovially, yet not overly seriously either. Just matter of fact. This is the way it was!

He did not minister to everyone; but there were hundreds, and each one saw 100 percent instant success. One person was skin and bones. I don't know what was wrong with him; some wasting disease. Inside of a couple seconds, he was the correct weight and grabbed at our feet.

Blind eyes fluttered open, ears popped open, startling the people. One person had pupil-less eyes, just white orbs in the sockets. Irises appeared, pupils shrunk in the bright sun. Mute tongues began singing the mighty praises of Jesus Christ, God of creation. Bones materialized, arms, legs, fingers, toes, eyeballs, tongues, entire organ systems. Scars disappeared. Tumors evaporated. Facial deformities were instantly made perfect. If there was one person healed of a particular ailment, there were a dozen.

Hundreds of miracles. I just…I can't even explain to you what I saw. All of what I just typed, when I read it, seems so weak compared to seeing it happen before my very eyes. How do I explain miracles on this level? Oh, Lord, show them!

What was so incredible was that as He would move through me, the people would see me, then see Him, then see me, then see Him shining forth. It was as if Jesus was phasing in and out, for lack of a better term, through me. Rather, He superimposed Himself over me. Over *everything*. There was no need for panorama, no need to even ask what was wrong. The Lord stood before them, and His overwhelming GLORY enveloped them, bowing them to the ground. When they stood, they were healed. No miracle took longer than twenty seconds.

I guess I'll stop now; I could go on for a hundred pages. I can't find a way to compare it, to explain it in English. Very rarely, if ever, since the times of Jesus and the early apostles has this level of miraculous power in manifestation been seen. But it's coming; I believe in this Dove Company, in this fullness of sonship anointing expression; and I am convinced the Lord will be manifested in a way not often seen since the Incarnation.

The commotion of Christ's fame reached a pandemonium level. For every miracle, a dozen people came to see what was going on. Most of them didn't even need prayer—they just wanted to see what God was accomplishing in His glory. They had heard He was there, doing what He did, and they came running. No celebrity was *this* famous, *this* well-known. God was here!

After a few hours, I was exhausted. I can't believe how much it took out of me just being with God. Flesh is so weak and inept.

I was outside the Lord now. People were jumping and clambering over each other, just to get a view of God. As I watched hundreds of people join in the tumult, He turned to me.

"Am I not God?" He asked me over the roar of the crowd. *"Am I not* **CREATOR***?!"* The word shook in the air, and the people whooped and praised Him, almost in a state of frenzy. *"Is there **anything** too difficult **for Me?**"*

And then I was back in my bed, in a sitting position, perspiring as if I'd run a marathon. I didn't just wake up like out of a pleasant dream. No. I couldn't catch my breath. I was utterly spent, and I flopped back down onto the bed—Jesus' words booming in my ears, my heart racing a mile a minute, *"Am I not Creator? Is there anything too difficult **for Me?**"*

I realized He'd placed extreme emphasis on the end of that statement: *"**for Me.**"* As in *God*, not *"for you"* as in James Maloney. I couldn't touch this, no matter how anointed I was, no matter how much I wanted it. It was Christ in me, manifesting Himself. The hope of glory.

And I knew the Holy Spirit was telling me something: I had to write this revelation down.

So here it goes…

2

HELPER

I TALKED A LITTLE BIT ABOUT THE AGGRESSIVE SIDE OF THE HOLY Spirit's help in my book, *The Dancing Hand of God*, specifically as He relates to us personally, internalized, to overcome our infirmities through the discernment of spirits operation. I further outlined this in *The Panoramic Seer*, operating in a prophetic anointing through the work of the Spirit to bring healing to others. But now I want to take a slightly different approach with a similar cut of cloth: that is, how the help of the aggressive side of the Holy Spirit is used to spread the fame of Jesus Christ through us as we manifest this sonship anointing.

I want to show a progression from personal, to ministerial, to end-time, radical expression, but not to demean any one type of particular flow, for it is all the same Spirit moving in different manifestations (see 1 Cor. 12:4). I believe one manifestation, for the premise of this book, builds on another, but that is not to imply a previous manifestation ceases to occur. All expressions are vital and necessary, for they all reveal the Lord through His Spirit; and I believe it is possible the penultimate expression of Christ (saving His physical return at "The End") through His people is in this sonship anointing, *expressing* Jesus, not simply *imitating* Jesus. I believe it is this type of manifestation that heralds the soon-coming Day of the Lord, the Third Great Awakening, the Army of the Lord, Third Pull of the Spirit—whatever term we'd like to use.

But who enables us for this manifestation of the Lord? Obviously something like this couldn't be initiated on our end.

> *Likewise the Spirit also helpeth our infirmities: for we know not what we should pray for as we ought: but the Spirit itself maketh intercession for us with groanings which cannot be uttered* (Romans 8:26 KJV).

Most of us probably have this verse memorized; it is oft-repeated in charismatic writings, and has had an excessive amount of in-depth study conducted on just what this verse is saying. If you've read my previous books, not only does that make you a well-versed friend of mine, but you might recall a bit about this scripture, for we discussed it at some length. But it's a good thing to take a bit here and reemphasize a couple of concepts about just what this Helper is helping us to do. So if this is rehash, forgive me. If it's not, memorize the following for the test at the end of the book. (That's a joke—there's no test.)

First, in the New King James, "itself" has been changed to "Himself." This is a correct retranslation in light of the full context of the Bible, even though the Greek word *pneuma* (Strong's #4151, "new-mah") by itself is gender-neutral. We should know that the Spirit is not an impersonal force, but a Being, very God Himself; and I think it is important to recognize His personal, living influence and communication with us, His children. He is not an It, some mystical wind or feeling, but rather a Person with whom we can have a relationship. The Spirit has a mind, will, and emotions (see Rom. 8:27; 15:30; Eph. 4:30). It is possible to anger Him (see Isa. 63:10); it is possible to reject Him (see Acts 7:51); it is possible to blaspheme Him (see Matt. 12:32). Not to mention the many verses that show the Spirit speaks (see about half a dozen references throughout the Book of Acts; Heb. 3:7-8; Rev. 2:7).

All of this is a very brief overview to show that the Spirit is indeed a Person who is given by the Lord Jesus Christ (see John 3:34) for this express purpose: to help in the plight against our infirmities (see John 14).

I want to point out the word "infirmities" (Strong's #769) is actually singular: "infirmity." It means the infirmity of our human condition. But it encompasses all the infirmities our "flesh" faces: physical, mental, emotional—specifically our inability to properly convey ourselves to God (that's the *"...for we know not what we should pray for..."* part). We're not sure exactly how to express what we are in need of to God—we just know that we need! We need (isn't that clever?) Someone to be able to convey what's lacking to the Father, Someone to show us what's missing—be that physical healing, moral ineptitude, or something mentally or emotionally "not right."

So the Spirit *helps* us. This is a ludicrously long Greek word: synantilambanomai (Strong's #4878), pronounced "soon-an-tee-lam-ba-no-my." (Imagine having to say all that just to ask for help?) It means "to take up our cause, to champion our case, to heave with us." It implies work on the Spirit's part, and ours. He helps us, not does it all for us. We can't sit back and expect Him to help us into laziness. Yet God realizes in our own power, with our human infirmity, it is impossible to accomplish the activities required to meet those needs, whatever they may be. We may strive, and have a measure of success, but to be more than a conqueror requires godly assistance.

Another super-long Greek word, *hyperentygchano* (Strong's #5241, pronounced "hoop-er-en-toong-khan-o"—*Gesundheidt!*) translates to "maketh intercession" in the previous scripture. You'll recognize "hyper" as in over and above, exceedingly much, like "hyperactive," "hypercritical" and "hyperbole." One of the concepts of the "tygchano" part speaks of an aggressive action, to throw oneself into the midst of. To make a case for or against someone (intercede on behalf of another, like a lawyer representing a defendant.) To alight upon, to fall upon. We can compare *tupto* (Strong's #5180) which means to "thump" or to strike out, to smack repeatedly, with a stick, with the palm of the hand, to collide, or to "smite."

The inference, then, that many theologians have made is "maketh intercession" means that our Helper, that glorious Intruder, over and above, exceedingly much, strikes out against our infirmity in an aggressive, angry manner. He is upset that this weakness of flesh plagues us and rises up to plead our case before the Father. Not just in a passive, demure, "Please help them," manner (and yes, He *does* do this) but also, "Help them *now!* Rip it away from them! Do it! Burn it up!" The Holy Spirit becomes enraged, after a fashion, at the circumstances that prohibit us from "helping" ourselves, and He lashes out against the infirmity, the weakness, striking it over and over, cudgeling it to pieces. "Maketh intercession" can mean "smashing" the infirmity on our behalf.

Let us also remember, it is the Spirit working *alongside* us (see John 14:16; Helper, Comforter, Counselor, *Parakletos*, Strong's #3875) with our effort, meager though it may be. As we struggle and strike out against our weakness, He backs us up and lends His strength to destroy it. More than any physical effort, it is as we yield to the Spirit that our "struggle" is strengthened by His righteous anger.

But let's also show the other side of the coin. While this book highlights the aggressive nature of the Spirit's help, we must also be balanced in recognizing that the Spirit is the great Comforter. According to the Amplified version of the Bible (see John 14:16; 14:26; 15:26), He is our Standby, our Advocate, our Strengthener. One called alongside, meaning to walk with us through the journey of life, to hold our hands if need be, to encourage and uplift, to mother us after a fashion. Not mollycoddle nor pander, not cosset nor pamper, but rather to inspire, enrich, improve and hearten our lives in the midst of difficulty and deprivation. The concept of

Parakletos conveys One who aids a needy person, One who is an *expert* in the field of ministering to another, bending over them and caring for them. Just as Jesus is our great Advocate in heaven (see 1 John 2:1) who ever lives to make intercession for us to the Father (see Heb. 7:25)—we also have an Intercessor and Advocate living within our spirits, inside our very bodies. And He comforts us in our needs.

And yet, He is seen as a *rushing mighty wind* as well as a dove. Let's not kid ourselves here, we're at war. Against an enemy called "average"—we fight against the nominal, the mundane. Mediocrity is rewarded in modern society, or at least I think so. If people set their sights low, they're not disappointed with setbacks and frustrations; too many coast along, going through the motions in their day-to-day lives and spiritual lives. This is sad; we are created for so much more than ordinariness.

That is the very definition of a religious spirit: one that honors God for what He did in the past, but fights against what He wants to do today! This kind of spirit wants us to maintain the status quo of existence; it wars against us to engage in the Spirit. It wants to sedate us into a numb acceptance of "almost experiences." "We almost had revival, we almost saw so-and-so healed, we almost prophesied in church this morning."

We need Someone to *throw* Himself into our case, to guide our prayers, to "interfere" (in a good way) with the affairs of humankind. We need to be shocked into awareness that the enemy wants us mollified, quelled—the Spirit wants us roaring like lions. So many of us in the Church want to be victorious in at least one area of our lives (you may be thinking dozens!), but I often find those same people do not want to be moved by the Spirit into a place of spiritual edginess and, dare I say, discomfort where we can see the "new-now" (fresh, exciting, and in-the-present) thing that God wants to do in our lives. And of course it is *just* that "new-now" thing that would solve the problem! But the flesh doesn't like change, so the Intruder "helps" our infirmity—even if that means "rubbing us the wrong way" from time to time. It's good to get your feathers ruffled on occasion!

INFIRMITY

Infirmity is a weakness, yes; but there are deeper definitions that the enemy wants to take advantage of so we might be kept placated, dormant, and docile. Infirmity is a limitation placed upon us by the enemy of our faith. The concept conveys the demonic (for that is what a religious spirit is) *spitting* on us, decreeing and prognosticating a constraint that keeps us bowed down. The most literal definition of "infirmity" is a "repeated whipping."

For example, the enemy will project an image (a word) based upon familiarity (this is what's called a "familiar spirit") of something known through your past generations. So like, in the physical realm, diabetes is an infirmity—a repeated whipping. The lie says it will be repeated in your life, if it happened in your mother's. Alcoholism is an infirmity. Skeletal fatigue, muscular degeneration, terminal illness. People who are invalids. (I give these as concrete examples of what we're talking about in the natural.) Those in a coma (and some of us, I'd venture to say, are *spiritually* comatose as well!). To be vexed by the demonic, to be plagued. Weakness, infirmity.

Spiritually and emotionally, the enemy spits out a veiling, a cloak of hopelessness and inevitability, deceiving us into believing that "things will always be the way they are." We cannot progress, we cannot overcome; better to batten down the hatches and tuck our heads under our pillows. Let's just sit this one out and do nothing.

Yuck…

It is a yoke, a weight, a load, a burden that doesn't permit you to stand up to your full height. That is infirmity. It could be a weakness of intimidation—sapping our boldness, our *chutzpah*, our *brio*, if I may wax poetic.

The enemy wants to bring you and me down into agreement with that infirmity, a *bonding* with the deficiency so that our bodies begin to reject our spirits.

> *For ye see your calling, brethren, how that not many wise men after the flesh, not many mighty, not many noble, are called: but God hath chosen the foolish things of the world to confound the wise; and God hath chosen the weak things of the world to confound the things which are mighty; and base things of the world, and things which are despised, hath God chosen, yea, and things which are not, to bring to nought things that are: that no flesh should glory in his presence* (1 Corinthians 1:26-29 KJV).

Base things, weak things, and foolish things (Strong's #36, #772, #3474). These words are interesting in the Greek. Base means of "low birth"—literally "no genes," *agenes*—cowardly, ignoble, of no reputable family. Weak is pretty accurate, "sickly, feeble, impotent, without strength." Foolish is "without learning," but the kicker is the derivative comes from "shut the mouth," as in lacking the ability to talk right—and is where we get the modern word "moron," someone with mental retardation or stunted faculties.

It's almost as if the Spirit is saying, "Without My help, you'd be a basket case, spiritually, physically, emotionally! You need help with these infirmities! You don't know what to do even in the smallest spiritual matter—you're like a moron!" He's not mocking us; He's pointing out that those "things" are turned around to the benefit of humankind, as was the "foolishness" of the crucifixion used to confound the wise, for the foolishness of God is greater than human wisdom. We're not called sheep for nothing! Sheep are not the brightest lamps in the clubhouse, you know? But the Shepherd takes care of the sheep; He helps us.

The Intruder's position is *alongside*. With us, "to take hold together against" our infirmities. And while there is the passive help of the Holy Spirit, the spiritual holding our hands and giving us a smooch, there is also an attitude of the Holy Spirit pertaining to righteous anger, even *rage*. One preacher termed it "the insanity of the Holy Spirit." The Spirit's desire is so passionate toward freeing us of our weaknesses that He refuses to let us go. He wraps Himself around our cause and says, "If this weakness doesn't let you go, I'll *rip* it away from you with My bare hands." Like a wild Man!

If you don't think the Holy Spirit is capable of becoming that demonstrative, just ask Ananias and Sapphira (see Acts 5). Note that Peter refers to their lying to and testing the *Spirit*, whom he calls God in verse 4. And also note that great fear (as in *awful reverence,* "dread, terror,"—fear, phobia, *megas phobos*, Strong's #3173 and #5401) came upon the church when Ananias and his wife died.

This isn't the Spirit slaying people at random out of temper, which is contrary to New Testament grace, because there is back story required to understand *why* Ananias and Sapphira breathed their last. Peter makes it clear they were under no compulsion to give *all* their proceeds of the sale of their possession, that it was up to them, since *"While it remained, was it not your own? And after it was sold, was it not in your own control?"* (Acts 5:4)—but rather because Ananias and his wife conspired to deceive the apostle and to test his authority in leading the saints. And why did they do so?

Even in the earliest stages of the Christian church, worldliness and mixture were trying to creep in. A catering to self-centeredness and fleshly desire. A demonic conspiracy of sorts was brewing in an effort to taint the simplicity and purity of the early Christians. It wanted to mix Christianity and its expression with the Greek and Roman pantheon of the day. As an example, especially the worship of Diana and Artemis (the goddess of virginity and the hunt) in the city of Ephesus. It was a very wicked and debauched cult in ancient times, and even still this false goddess is worshiped today by many neopagans and Wiccans.

A "NICOLAS SPIRIT"

This nefarious attempt to mix the saints has been termed a "Nicolas spirit."

Now before all the wonderful brethren out there named Nicolas get in an uproar, the name Nicolas is Greek, *Nikolaos* (Strong's #3532, from *Nike,* the goddess of victory, "to utterly vanquish," and *laos,* "the people," where we get the English word "laity"—this comes from the Greek *las,* "stone," supposedly from a legend that mankind was repopulated from stones after a great flood). Nicolas means to conquer the people, literally "I win people," or "I dominate over the conquered." Now we soften this today and say it means the "victor of the people" and this is sort of correct, but in truth the compound words convey the notion of "putting down the people."

In Acts 6:5, one of the original seven deacons was Nicolas of Antioch, a proselyte (meaning he converted from Roman paganism to Judaism) who became Christian. Early church leaders—Irenaeus, Hippolytus, Epiphanius—cite this Nicolas as starting a heretical cult preaching a mixture of Christianity and licentious behavior, extreme self-indulgence, smacking of Diana worship—if not in name, then certainly in the "spirit" of Diana. He taught it was okay to mix the occult practices with Judaism and Christianity, lumping it all together and not making a distinction with the purity of Christ's doctrine. What a dangerous proposition!

So much so that Jesus Himself denounced the doctrine of the Nicolaitans in Revelation 2:6, citing that the church of Ephesus (who had overcome Diana worship by the "special miracles" wrought through Paul's hands; see Acts 19:11) had at least one thing going for them: they hated the practice of Nicolaitism, which Jesus also hates. And yes, the word is "hate"—to find "completely disgusting." To loathe it with a fierce passion. To utterly reject. Jesus cannot abide mixture, for it muddles the spreading of His fame.

While we don't know beyond doubt that Ananias and Sapphira were literally followers of Nicolas, it is obvious this *mentality* of mixture was already creeping into the new disciples, for they were attempting to question Peter's authority in teaching the unadulterated word of Jesus Christ. Their actions were a challenge to his headship, and it's as if the people were standing back to see what would come of this move to test the authenticity of Peter's apostleship. Would Ananias and Sapphira get away with their hypocrisies?

Further, the notion of "nico-laity" is to keep the people held down in muck and mire, not permitting them to rise up and operate as Jesus intended them to operate: as a victorious, leading edge of human society. It says, "Be pacified in fleshly endeavor, be kept down; don't push toward the excellence of God's glory manifested through your lives; don't rise up into the perfection of the Holy Spirit's works in your life. Be content in the middle; don't excel."

Jesus *hates* this concept. There is a similar evil working in religiosity that attempts to keep the people quelled in a state of spiritual stupor. This is mixture as well, but it takes a "religious righteous" stance.

Jesus had warned the disciples, "*...Take heed, beware of the leaven of the Pharisees...*" (Mark 8:15). We know a little leaven leavens the whole lump according to Galatians 5:9. The Lord perceived that even then a religious spirit was threatening to try to asphyxiate the coming move of the Spirit, and He cautioned those like Peter, the fathers of His new church, to be wary of the legalistic wiles of a spirit that seeks to stifle *the* Spirit's flow among the saints.

Thankfully, Peter had paid attention to Christ's admonition, for there was a clique among the saints who were *testing* the leadership of Peter. Those who were waiting to see if the apostle could be tricked or manipulated (in other words, would Ananias and

Sapphira get away with it?). If Peter had allowed the deception to "slide," it would've opened the way for the leaven to leaven (odd phrase) the whole group. This had to be nipped in the bud, the factionalism that threatened the unity of the congregation, the *"one accord in Solomon's Porch"* (Acts 5:12).

Peter was protecting the flock, as a pastor should. And while it is tremendously sad that two people died, this act sheltered the thousands of new converts from religious and worldly leaven, at least for a time. Note: I am not saying God *killed* Ananias and Sapphira, nor will I make any kind of statement concerning where their spirits went when they breathed their last—all I am saying is that the Lord permitted this situation to occur; and yes, it was a chastening circumstance, but it protected the sanctity and purity of the Spirit flowing through the church, and specifically through Peter.

I've taken time for this little bunny trail in Acts 5 because there is a somewhat alarming teaching I've heard that some ministers are putting forth: that Peter superseded or abused his apostolic authority in the case of Ananias and Sapphira concerning the "keys of the kingdom" that Jesus gave to the apostle in Matthew 16:19 (i.e., the authority to bind and to loose: what is allowed on earth is allowed in heaven, what is not permitted on earth is not permitted in heaven—rather, that God backs up the words of His children). I disagree wholeheartedly with this notion that Peter surpassed his authority.

The original apostles, including Peter, walked in a deeper revelation than any who have come since. We must make this distinction, for it is generally recognized that twelve of the twenty-four thrones in Revelation 4:4 represent the apostles, the other twelve represent the tribes of Israel. Even if this point were argued, at the very least, the wall of the New Jerusalem, homeplace for the bride of Christ, has twelve foundation stones inscribed with the names of the original apostles (see Rev. 21:14). Thus, the foundation of the Church is, indeed, built upon the apostles (and prophets) with Christ Himself being the chief Cornerstone (see Eph. 2:20).

We cannot forget that Peter walked with the Lord during His earthly ministry, seeing firsthand with his very own natural eyes how Jesus ministered in the authority of binding and loosing. As such, the early apostles must be sacrosanct in the execution of their authority and revelation, for indeed, we have most of the New Testament through their hands. They are inviolable concerning their manifestation of authority to hear from the Spirit and operate under the influence of that same Spirit. That doesn't make them "perfect"—for they weren't—but their *revelation* and the implementation of that revelation cannot be contested.

> *Truly the signs of an apostle were accomplished among you with all perseverance, in signs and wonders and mighty deeds* (2 Corinthians 12:12).

You probably know that "signs" in this Second Corinthians 12:12 verse is *semeion* (Strong's #4592, "say-my-on"), which derives from *sema*, meaning "be it here known," an indication to signify something. It was an official mark, a signet or seal, used to authenticate a ruling by the courts. The stamp of approval, the guarantee of authenticity that "this is the real deal, we're not even playing here."

It was these kinds of signs that followed the apostles' deeds, and this includes Peter, whom no one questions that he was, indeed, an apostle of the Lord Jesus Christ. Does this sound like the kind of person who can operate without the mark of God's approval upon his life? Is it possible for him to "miss it"? I daresay not.

After the incident with Ananias and Sapphira, Acts 5:16 shows the continuing grace and power of the church, and Peter especially. So much so, even his *shadow* exudes the authority to heal. This was the "greater works" Christ was talking about in John 14:12. How could this be the case if Peter had exceeded his apostolic parameters?

No, rather, Peter was acting under the discerning revelation of the Holy Spirit, who had shown him the subtle plot that was undergirding Ananias and Sapphira's deception and *testing*. And what were they testing? The apostle's discernment, and ergo, his ability to hear from the Spirit. Ultimately the Spirit Himself. It wasn't just the withholding of the proceeds or their individual deception (that could be forgiven); it was the spiritual ramifications that were attempting to sow disunity among the saints, allowing a mixture to enter the congregation, be it from a worldly Nicolas spirit or a religious Pharisaical spirit.

The Holy Spirit, in His sovereignty, couldn't permit that leaven to enter the flock; He was protecting the larger group of the saints in revealing to Peter the conspiracy being set forth. The outcome of that revelation was permitted by the Spirit; and sad as it was, it brought greater unity to the core group of saints.

Now of course you and I have no need to fear the Spirit in quite that measure! We have no intentions of sabotaging His sons. But I think we would be wise not to test His limits of grace and mercy. Let us not forget He is the *Holy* Spirit (*hagios*, Strong's #40, sacred, most holy, from *hagos*, "an awful thing" as in awe-full). Reverence (not fear of reprisal or punishment) is never a bad thing! Truly the fear of the Lord is the beginning of knowledge and wisdom (see Prov. 1:7; 9:10; Ps. 111:10).

But, now back to our Helper, the glorious Intruder, who is quite capable of helping us in the aggressive sense.

To what purpose? That we might be free of our infirmity, in whatever fashion that may be, a physical illness, an emotional hindrance, a mental blockage; so that in turn, we might display, manifest, and exhibit not just a semblance of our Lord's triumphant expression, but His very Being shining through us. Thus is His fame spread far and wide throughout the earth.

I am not talking about *becoming* God—that is heresy. I am talking about overcoming (hyper-putting down) *self* and *ego* so that the God who lives inside us might work through us as He sees fit, in His measure of anointing and power (not ours), in His limitless, explosive expression that sets fire to the world, releasing passion and fervor for becoming more like Him in every facet of life. That we might know Him! That we might so blend our desires and actions with His that He is literally manifested through us; we become the *sons* of God. Our hands become His hands to work as He does; our eyes become as His eyes to see things the way they really are; our movement becomes His movement to set the captives free. This is what creation eagerly waits for (again, see Rom. 8:19).

Permit me to quote Charles Spurgeon in sharing an example he gave on the intercession of the Holy Spirit:

> Yet one more illustration: it is that of *a father aiding his boy*. Suppose it to be a time of war centuries back. Old English warfare was then conducted by bowmen to a great extent. Here is a youth who is to be initiated in the art of archery, and therefore he carries a bow. It is a strong bow, and therefore very hard to draw; indeed, it requires more strength than the urchin can summon to bend it. See how his father teaches him. "Put your right hand here, my boy, and place your left hand so. Now pull"; and as the youth pulls, his father's hands are on his hands, and the bow is drawn. The lad draws the bow: ay, but it is quite as much his father, too. We cannot draw the bow of prayer alone. Sometimes a bow of steel is not broken by our hands, for we cannot even bend it; and then the Holy Ghost puts his mighty hand over ours, and covers our weakness so that we draw; and lo, what splendid drawing of the bow it is then! The bow bends so easily we wonder how it is; away flies the arrow, and it pierces the very centre of the target, for he who giveth the strength directeth the aim. We rejoice to think that we have won the day, but it was his secret might that made us strong, and to him be the glory of it.[1]

Let's refer again to John 14:15-18, wherein Jesus is talking about this Comforter, the Spirit of truth, the glorious Intruder being sent to help us. In the King James, verse 18 says, *"I will not leave you comfortless...."* but the New King James renders this more succinctly as *"I will not leave you orphans..."* since the Greek word is *orphanos* (Strong's #3737). Contrast being an orphan, one bereaved of parents, to John 1:12, *"But as many as received Him, to them He gave the right to become children of God, to those who believe in His name."* We have inherited an entire family represented in one God: our Father; our older Brother, Friend, and Lord (see Prov. 18:24; John 15:13-15; Rom. 8:15), who is the firstborn Son (see Rom. 8:29); and a Spirit called alongside so we will not be comfortless until we see our Brother and Father face to face.

Let us identify what it means to be a "son." As you might know, the Greek word is *huios* (Strong's #5207, "hwe-oss"), and it denotes one whom God "esteems, loves, protects and benefits above others"— referring specifically to Christians in the New Testament. One who is obedient to God, receptive of loving chastisements so that His children—sons and daughters—might be shaped by the Father (see Heb. 12:5-8) to be conformed in the image of His Son (again, see Rom. 8:29).

"Image" is *eikon* (Strong's #1504, aptly enough where we get the English word "icon"), and means "likeness, of moral excellence, not just in a future heavenly body, but of a 'renewed mind' on this earth," and thereby *given the power to command.* The concept of being iconic in the biblical sense is to create in a person the authority to command, hold sway, rule in dominion; it is the power to decree a thing (see Job 22:28) and have it established as so, because we have the right (entitlement, privilege, justification, merit, birthright) to speak on behalf of our Father, through Jesus, by the aid of the Spirit.

A son has the inherited right to act in the father's stead in the case of his absence, meaning our Father is not visibly present on this earth (of course, we know He is omnipresent and "here" with us always—for God is *everywhere;* see Jeremiah 23:23-24. Just as Jesus is; see Matthew 28:20). We are not servants or illegitimate by-products of unholy union; we are not aliens in the house of God. We are sons, and as such we are given the right and authority to act just as if the Father was standing there; for by the help of the Spirit, we have the mind of Christ (see 1 Cor. 2:16) and can know exactly how the Father would act (see John 5:19).

Therefore, to manifest Jesus, *the* Son, as sons, is to ensure the Father's will is executed just as He would like it, with no variance. This is what all of creation cries out for! This is what the Helper aggressively pursues in His intercession for us, as He leads us (see Rom. 8:14) through our times before the Father: that we step into our rightful place as sons and make Jesus *famous* throughout the world.

Let's identify what is meant by the *fame* of God.

Endnote

1. Charles Haddon Spurgeon, *The Metropolitan Tabernacle Pulpit: Sermons*; #1532 (April 11, 1880), 222-223.

3

ASTONISHED

And when the ark of the covenant of the Lord came into the camp,
all Israel shouted so loudly that the earth shook. Now when the
Philistines heard the noise of the shout, they said, "What does the
*sound of this **great shout** in the camp of the Hebrews mean?" Then*
they understood that the ark of the Lord had come into the camp.
So the Philistines were afraid, for they said, "God has come into
the camp!" And they said, "Woe to us! For such a thing has never
happened before. Woe to us! Who will deliver us from the hand of
these mighty gods? These are the gods who struck the Egyptians
with all the plagues in the wilderness" (1 Samuel 4:5-8).

These were the sounds of deliverance, yes? The mighty shout of the
Israelites. We know the ark represents the manifest presence of the
Lord, His glory went with it. And as it was restored into the camp,
an extravagant response came forth. One that shook the earth! This
violent reaction created a stir among the enemy; fear fell upon the
Philistines. They acknowledged that God was in their midst!

See, God wants to be experienced. I will always remain uncon-
vinced that the Lord intended people to follow Him without ever
experiencing His divine presence in a tangible, physical way. The
scriptures just don't show that. It's sad when His children are taught

that He is some untouchable force up there in the cosmos, and we all have to wait till we die to meet Him.

Christianity is not *just* something we're supposed to know (and yes, we are supposed to *know*, don't misunderstand), but it's something we're also supposed to feel. As the manifest presence of God is restored (by that I mean, experienced through our five senses; see Heb. 5:14), unusual reactions and responses will come forth. This is how the fame of Jesus is spread. People will be *shocked* into awareness that He is a real Being and He desires to interact with His sons and daughters. What a privilege, what a duty! We *must* be moved on by the Holy Spirit in a way that releases these shouts of deliverance to shake up the enemy's camps.

What kind of unusual reactions am I talking about here? Some might be extravagant praise, or militant intercession—warring in tongues, groaning in the Spirit, travail, shouting, laughter, crying. I'm okay with all of that. These are natural responses to supernatural stimuli. These are the aggressive moves of the Spirit, and they should be heartfelt and intense, soul-shaking. And I'm not endorsing that we swing like monkeys from the chandeliers or howl at the moon, but I do think one of the purposes of the glory is to elicit some kind of a response.

God responds to those kinds of reactions. For example, *"Elijah was a man with a nature like ours, and he prayed earnestly that it would not rain; and it did not rain on the land for three years and six months. And he prayed again, and the heaven gave rain, and the earth produced its fruit"* (James 5:17-18). It was based on Elijah's fervent prayer that elicited God's response of withholding rain, and releasing it once again. As we emote, God emotes and vice versa.

That word *fervency* is pretty neat. It means "having or showing great emotion or warmth, to be ardent, fiery, fervid, zealous, to be extremely hot." In fact, it comes from the Latin, "boiling hot, glowing." It is an extreme emotion in response to the presence of God. It's this kind of prayer that "availeth much."

Speaking of our Lord, *"who, in the days of His flesh, when He had offered up prayers and supplications, with vehement cries and tears to Him who was able to save Him from death, and was heard because of His godly fear"* (Heb. 5:7). Jesus travailed in His soul. We are talking about crying loudly, shrieking out, screaming—vehement cries and tears.

The point of all this is to say that spreading the fame of Jesus, through the overwhelming help of the Holy Spirit, stems from *experiencing* the manifest presence of God, something tangibly felt, seen, heard, touched, or tasted in our bodies that brings about a sense of shock and astonishment.

There is an imprint of God that remains from these kinds of encounters—they stay with you for life. Have you ever pondered what that phrase means, "in the Spirit" (like in Rev. 1:10, and others)? Experiencing the militant, aggressive influence of the Spirit is one way of looking at it. Yes, experiencing the gentle doveness (not a real word), but also the roaring lion nature of the Spirit. It is how one sees things from God's perspective, by being carried away in the Spirit—whether bodily or spiritually. It means to be caught up in an experience with Him. It is the sign of the imprint and influence of God that *elevates us* out of our natural surroundings. To be caught away. May we even say, *entranced* by Him? I think we'll show that's a correct definition.

See, we need these kinds of encounters if we're to be His manifested sons. We need to enter into the word as it is being spoken (the *rhema* that's being *phero'*d, I mean)—again, that comingling of the Word and the Spirit. What I mean by *rhema* that's *phero'*d is that as we dwell in the scriptures, the Spirit prophetically breathes on them, making them present and alive. A concept from the Word that is quickened by the Spirit in the *now*. There is an element of the prophetic involved in these experiences. It's not just receiving a word, as important as that is; but rather, it is a release of *the* Word (Jesus Himself) being made flesh to us (see John 1:14), being manifested as a reality. That's one of the main purposes of the prophetic—to lead people into these kinds of transcendent encounters. This is what Revelation 19:10 is saying, *"For the testimony of Jesus is the spirit of prophecy."* Spreading the fame of Jesus is directly tied to these encounters *in* Jesus, through being *in* the Spirit, but "in the Spirit" *in the present, in reality.* (That's a lot of ins.) Not just as a concept or vague idea, but a real happening that we can palpably experience.

The people in the world need to have those experiences translated to them as well. To be shocked by the Spirit; there's such a dearth of expression in most people's lives, Christian or otherwise. People are thirsty for the word of the Lord, that word that initiates a "caught-up" meeting with God Himself.

> *"Behold, the days are coming," says the Lord God, "that I will send a famine on the land, not a famine of bread, nor a thirst for water, but of hearing the words of the Lord"* (Amos 8:11).

Recovering, or recapturing, and expressing the testimony of Jesus through the spirit of prophecy is what satisfies the famine. It is through these means that people are shocked into (higher) awareness of Almighty God.

> *Then they* [Jesus and Simon, Andrew, James and John] *went into Capernaum, and immediately on the Sabbath He entered the synagogue and taught. And they were* **astonished** *at His teaching, for He taught them as one having authority, and not as the scribes. Now there was a man in their synagogue with an unclean spirit. And he cried out, saying, "Let us alone! What have we to do with You, Jesus of Nazareth? Did You come to destroy us? I know who You are—the Holy One of God!" But Jesus rebuked him, saying, "Be quiet, and come out of him!" And*

*when the unclean spirit had convulsed him and cried out with a loud voice, he came out of him. Then they were all **amazed**, so that they questioned among themselves, saying, "What is this? What new doctrine is this? For with authority He commands even the unclean spirits, and they obey Him." **And immediately His fame spread throughout all the region around Galilee*** (Mark 1:21-28).

There are several Greek words here we need to highlight. I hope you enjoy these word studies because they take quite a bit of research and really do illuminate the individual words of the verses. Plus, I think they're fun!

First, "astonished" is *ekplesso* (Strong's #1605, "ek-play-so") and it means to be struck. I mean, literally *smacked,* "to strike one out of self-possession." To be struck amazed, astonished, panicked. It comes from the root "to smite." Paraphrased, coldcocked and rendered dazed.

Second, "amazed" is *thambeo* (Strong's #2284, "(th)om-bay-oh") and it can carry the connotation of being frightened, or even terrified, by what was seen, shocked into silence. The root comes from "to dumbfound" and "to render immovable"—that is, glued to the spot because you're so stunned by what you've seen and heard. Staggered, flabbergasted, astounded.

You'll notice these words in the Greek are a little stronger than our English "astonished" and "amazed."

"Fame" is pretty cool too. We've already given a decent definition of fame regarding the glory of God manifested, *doxa,* and so on. The Greek word itself is *akoe* (Strong's #189, "ah-kuh-a," where the A is long as in "hay"). It means "hearsay, report, rumor." Really, "what was heard," and can actually refer to the sense of hearing itself or the organ of hearing (the ear). So, "a thing has come to my ears"— in this case, about Jesus casting out the demon. Today we would say, "Hey, check this out. Guess what I just heard?"

Now, there's a bunch of Hebrew words in the Old Testament that are more or less accurately translated "fame." One means "voice, sound, noise," (Strong's #6963)—a proclamation—and is also the word translated "thunder" or "thunderings" in the Old Testament. It implies, "I've got your attention."

Another word means "a report, something heard" (Strong's #8088). It comes from a root meaning "to summon, to hear, to listen, to obey," and has a sister word (Strong's #8089) that is translated "fame" in Joshua 6:27 and 9:9 and means "a [noised] report." It has another sister word virtually identical (Strong's #8052) that is the "bruit" of Jeremiah 10:22 (KJV), which is an archaic, Old French way of saying "noisy"—racket, clamor, clang, din, roar, a cacophony.

The point I wish to convey is that fame is "loud"—it arrests the attention of the listeners. It is something heard with our own two ears. It's a noisy report that is flung far and wide. It is an *experience.*

But my favorite Hebrew word for "fame" is *shem* (Strong's #8034, "shame"). It literally means "name" and is one of the more common Jewish designations for God, "the Name." Fame and God are synonymous. It conveys renown, glory, a monument or memorial. One who is in a "conspicuous, definite position." High and lifted up (see Isa. 6:1). One firmly set or ordained as a sign, established, constituted, fixed, planted, set in place. A Name above all names.

> *And being found in appearance as a man, He humbled Himself and became obedient to the point of death, even the death of the cross. Therefore God also has highly exalted Him and given Him **the name which is above every name**, that at the name of Jesus every knee should bow, of those in heaven, and of those on earth, and of those under the earth, and that every tongue should confess that Jesus Christ is Lord, to the glory of God the Father (Philippians 2:8-11).*

> *For unto us a Child is born, unto us a Son is given; and the government will be upon His shoulder. And His name will be called*

Wonderful, Counselor, Mighty God, Everlasting Father, Prince of Peace (Isaiah 9:6).

In a word: *famous.* And we have the distinct privilege and mandate to spread that fame to the farthest flung corners of the earth!

Okay, now one more Greek word here, and then you can switch back to normal English. This is the best one of all, and really conveys what I mean by "shocked" in the Spirit.

At times in the New Testament the words "amazed" or "astonished" (or variations thereof) are also the same word for "trance." This super-cool Greek word is *ekstasis* (Strong's #1611, "ex-stuh-sis"). You'll recognize this as the English words "ecstasy" or "ecstatic." (We steal a lot of words in English.) It is the noun form of the verb *existemi* (Strong's #1839, "ex-is-tay-me").

Being caught up in the Spirit is being entranced into an ecstatic experience with God. The word means "throwing the mind out of its normal state." Yes, it can mean an altered state of consciousness, but this is a dangerous term to throw around without knowing the *context* of rapture in God. The experience is about as far different from the New Age concept of trance as day is from night. The term can also mean "out of one's mind" in the sense of insane; but again, we're discussing something wholly different. We are talking about a sense of overcoming shock and amazement, an emotional and physical response to the manifested presence of God, initiated by the Holy Spirit.

RAPTUROUS ECSTASY

We are discussing being overcome by an experience to the point of being transported out of oneself into a state of rapture—"a blended state of fear and wonderment" where we are totally consumed by God and placed outside ourselves. Literally it means "to stand beside oneself" in amazement and astonishment. Shocked and stunned into a sublime experience with the glorious Intruder. A transcendent God sharing a transcendent moment with us. Our bodies are overwhelmed by the Spirit and we enter into a heightened state of spiritual awareness, open to revelation from that same Spirit.

When prophets and apostles in the Bible say they had visions, were in the Spirit, went into a trance, this is what they are talking about: rapturous ecstasy. A supernaturally instilled excitement of the physical body that is expressed through the five senses. God is experienced by seeing, hearing, feeling, tasting, and smelling. It goes beyond knowing God in our minds, and that is important as well; but this is the tangible evidence of His presence, and it brings us into a state of astonishment.

This is what happened to the people in Mark's Gospel, and this is why the Lord's fame spread. They encountered an uplifting, ecstatic experience and went around telling others about it. This is the work of the Spirit in our lives, to bring us into these encounters that are in turn converted to those around us, spreading the fame (noise, report, experience) of Jesus Christ. It takes these ecstatic moves of the Spirit operating in our lives, and we must yield to them, we must take hold the realm of the Spirit. When the presence of God is manifested, the glory, the Spirit will lead us into these kinds of "lifting up" experiences.

Now lest you think I'm sharing esoteric psychobabble with no scriptural basis, I bet you'd like some biblical references, huh? Good for you. Ready? Underline the following in your Bible: Matthew 12:23; Mark 2:12, 5:42, 6:51, 16:8; Luke 2:47, 5:26, 8:56; Acts 2:7, 3:10, 8:13, 10:10, 11:5, 22:17; 2 Corinthians 5:13, 12:3; and Revelation 1:10, 1:17.

There was precedent for trancelike encounters with God in the Old Testament as the Spirit would come upon people. Cases of "the Lord's hand" coming upon one, fear and trembling falling on one, a sudden power falling on prophets, falling into a deep sleep, having visions, etc. See Genesis 15:12; Numbers 24:4; Job 4:14, 33:15; Ezekiel 1:3, 3:14, 8:1, 11:24, 43:5; and Daniel 8:18, 10:7.

As always, we must exercise caution and balance, cultivating a discernment of spirits to test the fruit of such encounters, for the devil would like nothing more than to distract us with phony experiences created from our mind's eye or emotional outburst. The bottom line is, these kinds of experiences must always be initiated by the Spirit. I do not buy into the notion that we can "create" these experiences for ourselves, in the sense of "making up" an encounter in our mind's eye and then the Lord will make it actual. I believe that by doing so, we can open up ourselves to deception and "weirdness," trafficking in the demonic, or at the very least, catering to the flesh.

These are to be spiritual encounters originated by the glorious Intruder, being overwhelmed by the Spirit. We cannot force these things. However, we can place ourselves in a position to experience the Spirit in this fashion, by wholeheartedly seeking the Lord, praying in the Spirit, being with Him in the secret place—and from there, genuine encounters will commence.

These are not supposed to be casual, chance meetings with the Spirit. It is supposed to be a lifestyle with our Helper, stemming from a vibrant relationship with the Lord, being taken from glory to glory (see 2 Cor. 3:18), transformed into the very representation of our dear Lord, so His fame might spread.

In order for us to cultivate that kind of relationship, we must permit ourselves to be taken to a place where His Spirit is *resting* on us, not merely popping in for a quick intoxication moment and then flitting off. He must become a permanent mainstay in our day-to-day life. We must allow Him to intrude upon our lives.

> *Arise, shine; for your light has come! And the glory of the Lord is risen upon you. For behold, the darkness shall cover the earth, and deep darkness the people; but the Lord will arise over you, and His glory will be seen upon you. The Gentiles shall come*

to your light, and kings to the brightness of your rising (Isaiah 60:1-3).

That's another well-known passage most of us probably have memorized. What's it talking about? Among other things, the harvest, the influx of humanity into the kingdom of light. Why do they come? Because His glory is seen in us, His sons. This is that "common salvation," the faith for which we are earnestly contending (see Jude 1:3). It can't be done in our own strength. It takes the might of the Intruder, the Spirit of glory, resting overwhelmingly upon us so that we might bear the glory of God to the world.

> *If you are reproached for the name of Christ, blessed are you, for the Spirit of glory and of God rests upon you. On their part He is blasphemed, but on your part He is glorified* (1 Peter 4:14).

You most likely know that *glory* is the reputation of God in action; it is what causes His fame to be spread throughout the earth. The Hebrew word for "glory" is *kabowd* (Strong's #3519; sometimes transliterated *chabod)* and is pronounced "kah-voad." It figuratively means "weighty" (see the root in Strong's #3513) and speaks to riches, abundance, honor, and *reputation;* world-renown; the "fame" of God.

Glory can be defined as the weightiness of His limitless power and self-worth being manifested through His people. God's honor, omnipotent capability, and creativity in motion; His intrinsic wealth and value on display; His eminence (and immanence) and dignity perceived by humanity; His renown and prominence; His distinction and illustriousness—His very radiance shining forth.

Wow, that's a pretty awesome definition!

The Greek word for "glory" is *doxa* (Strong's #1391; reference the "Doxology"). It means to "have a good opinion of someone," in this case the Lord. Like *kabowd*, it speaks to reputation and majesty, stemming from an archaic verb "to expose to one's eyes"—to *show*—(see Strong's #1166). When referring to the Lord's brilliance, His manifested glory, *doxa* speaks of His visible splendor and brightness: we could say that it means "to shine"! In fact, *doxa* can speak of the luminosity of the heavenly bodies and the angelic. So how much more so, when the *doxa* of God Himself is shown to the world's eyes? He burns brighter than the sun before our vision, and we can't but throw our arms over our faces in the intensity of such shine!

Glory is the visible splendor of God that can be perceived through our five senses—a manifestation of His substance and significance on the earthly plane! But let's take this further as it pertains to you and me, His sons. The glory weighs down upon us and impresses the very honor and favor of Lord God Almighty through our actions. It stems from our *acceptance* by God. There is a chapter dedicated to this acceptance in my book, *The Dancing Hand of God*, for further study.

But for now, let us look at our acceptance in Him as if He was saying, "This is My opinion *(doxa)* of how I see you through My Son," and thus, His glory resonates, or rather gleams, through us. God looks at us, His children, as ones being *transformed* by the life of Christ and the help of the Spirit, and entrusts His very reputation, His fame, to our hands. That's a massive responsibility we should not take lightly! But if we allow the glorious Intruder to *fill* us, to *rest* upon and overwhelm us, then the glory of the Lord will be *seen* on us!

Can I share a few compelling reasons for allowing the Spirit to intrude upon your life?

First, an infusion of supernatural energy. I know all about fatigue, and let's be honest, a lot of us are bone-weary. It's not even just physical tiredness; many of us are plagued by *mental* exhaustion. We can't even think straight! But the pervasive resting, glorious Intruder demolishes the infirmities of enervation. When He comes upon you and stays upon you, He obliterates depression and mental prostration. He physically and mentally lifts us into the realm of joy and strength, radically attacking the adverse circumstances that beat us down.

Lest you think I'm making this up, allow me to point out Isaiah 60:1, this time from the Amplified Bible. *"Arise [from the depression and prostration in which circumstances have kept you—rise to a new life]! Shine (be radiant with the glory of the Lord), for your light has come, and the glory of the Lord has risen upon you!"*

Gloom corrodes our logical thought processes; it ferments our creative juices. Our brains are pickled.

Yet the glory of the Lord is come, *"To console those who mourn in Zion, to give them beauty for ashes, the oil of joy for mourning, the garment of praise for the spirit of heaviness; that they may be called trees of righteousness, the planting of the Lord, that He may be glorified"* (Isa. 61:3).

The anointing of God's glory comes upon His sons, through Jesus and the resting of His Spirit, so that we might be *glad* and not morose. There is no room for morbid misery. We are *in* Christ, remember. And what was said of Him? *"You love righteousness and hate wickedness; therefore God, Your God, has anointed You with the oil of gladness more than Your companions"* (Ps. 45:7).

> *...Go your way, eat the fat, drink the sweet, and send portions to those for whom nothing is prepared; for this day is holy to our Lord. Do not sorrow, for the joy of the Lord is your strength* (Nehemiah 8:10).

This supernatural influx of glory is God's response to the moral darkness and dejection, the pervasive pessimism and murkiness that covers the world. We wade through melancholy and shadows of despondency. Let's be honest, many people are unhappy; their lives seem dreary to them. But the glory of the Lord coming upon His manifested sons provides the *victory over* this "deep darkness"!

Indeed, arise and shine! For Gentiles, kings will come to the brightness of our rising as the Spirit of glory smothers the futility of our minds, the darkened understanding that stems from ignorance and blindness (see Eph. 4:17-18).

In the consistent resting of the glorious Intruder upon us, we see His *explosive* intervention in the gross darkness of mental "droopiness" (I suppose the word *ennui* might fit; lethargic apathy and moral ambivalence). But there is also a *peaceful* intervention, a return to a state of bliss and harmony. I think both these interventions are represented in the "great power" and "great grace" of Acts 4:33.

> *And He said, "My Presence will go with you, and I will give you rest"* (Exodus 33:14).

In the resting of the Spirit, there is rest for us. Selah. The rest of faith means finding rest in the midst of activity. To have ubiquitous peace while we labor, because we know *"the chastisement for our peace was upon Him…"* (Isa. 53:5).

"There remains therefore a rest for the people of God" (Heb. 4:9). This rest is a place of faith in which you and I are to function. In it is the absence of overbearing stress and conflict, turmoil, tensions, and hassles. Rest is the supernatural ability to function at full capacity and strength all the while sustained by an in-working, an inward strengthening fed by the Spirit of glory.

> *"You therefore, my son, be strong in the grace that is in Christ Jesus"* (2 Timothy 2:1).

Besides the rest of faith, there is a rest in strength. Just as Samson rose up and killed the lion (see Judg. 14:5-6), the Spirit rests upon us to renew our strength inwardly.

"My glory is fresh within me, and my bow is renewed in my hand" (Job 29:20). In Job's time, the bow was a weapon used for military purposes, for gathering food—people lived by the bow. What this verse is saying is while setting the bow, for it to be renewed in the hand, meant the archer was getting stronger and stronger. Stringing a bow took a great deal of exertion and energy; it was time consuming. But as the glory maintained its freshness, it became easier and easier to nock an arrow. Job was saying ordinarily he would've been completely worn out, but God's glory, His honor manifested, refreshed him. He was getting stronger while exerting energy, not weaker. His bow was renewed, changed, in his hand.

This means we can function in life and not be overly fatigued in our everyday activity! So as we use our faith and use our strength, the Helper provides a rest in the midst of labor; but we cannot rely only on our own limited reservoirs of strength; rather, we must look to the Intruder to infuse His glory with ours. As we yield ourselves to the Spirit's resting, our endurance is built.

Yes, there is an endurance in faith; *"When Gideon came to the Jordan, he and the three hundred men who were with him crossed over, exhausted but still in pursuit"* (Judg. 8:4). From a particular standpoint, "fatigue" can improve our performance. Just as athletes draw on that hidden well of strength, past the point of normal tiredness, to finish the game, to make the score, to win the race; we, too, by the help of the Holy Spirit can experience a spiritual "second wind" to finish the task before us. We move from a point of reason, to a point of instinct. For us, like Gideon's three hundred, we have no other choice but to continue pursuit. Throwing in the towel is not an option we should be willing to accept!

We need Gideon's mentality! Win. At all costs. Bring in the harvest, manifest the Lord; don't back away in intimidation—smite the ground in faith! (See 2 Kings 13.) We may be exhausted, but we're still in pursuit with victory in sight! This is the resting of the glorious Intruder. From the *"beginning of the year to the very end of the year"* (Deut. 11:12), He keeps us in special consideration; *"as your days, so shall your strength be"* (Deut. 33:25). We can make the statement in faith, by the help of the Holy Spirit, "I'm equal to the demands put upon me!"

In Daniel's famous vision, he makes the statement regarding the different king who subdues three kings and speaks pompous words against God that he *"shall persecute the saints of the Most High"* (Dan. 7:25). That word "persecutes" is literally "wear out" or run ragged. In these end times, we the saints must stand in endurance so we don't become haggard, faded, gaunt. This endurance comes from the resting of the Spirit of glory flowing out of us and coming upon us to *satisfy our thirst* for the manifest presence of God.

If the Holy Spirit starts releasing a trickle of inward joy in your life, and if you respond correctly by releasing that measure, it will then turn into a mighty river of joy.

People are dragging, thirsty, *parched* because Jesus is not made real to them! His sons must arise, must manifest the Lord in a saturating way.

It is *"by reason of use"* (Heb. 5:14) that our spiritual senses are exercised to discern both good and evil. We have *"tasted the heavenly gift, and have become partakers of the Holy Spirit"* (Heb. 6:4), but when He moves upon us, we must meet Him with a response! If the Lord moves us to joy, or peace, or even conviction—it does not have the necessary impact unless we *respond*. These experiences of the Spirit are to flow out of our hearts like a *mighty river*—what we have experienced for ourselves in the Spirit of glory coming upon us, in turn, is to be promoted to the people at large. God must be made real to them!

If this reality of the glorious Intruder is "dried up" or downplayed, the people can drift into the counterfeit, the occult deception, or turn to dead dry, ritualistic religious rote (that's a lot of alliteration!) and fermentation that won't satisfy the thirst for the true presence of God. We *must* have the Spirit resting upon us, and we must turn that experience outward to others!

The Spirit coming upon us will enable us to bring about a miraculous demonstration that will confirm the gospel. *"This beginning of signs Jesus did in Cana of Galilee, and manifested His glory; and His disciples believed in Him"* (John 2:11). The glory of God is manifested by the miraculous demonstration of the Spirit!

Note in Acts 2, it was the sound that drew the multitude together, as well as what they saw—a visible and audible manifestation of the Spirit, done in the open for all to see, as a sign to the unbelievers (see 1 Cor. 14:22). Some believed, and yes, some mocked. But see, tongues represent the operations and activity of the Holy Spirit who intrudes upon people's false or misguided conceptions by expressing and releasing freedom in the Body.

So, for the resting of the Spirit, we cannot underestimate the importance of speaking in tongues, which we explore in the next chapter.

4

TONGUES

I THINK MOST PEOPLE WHO KNOW ME A LITTLE BIT, EITHER through seeing my ministry or reading my books, know that I'm a big proponent of speaking in tongues. I've dedicated entire sections of teachings on heavenly prayer languages, addressing some distressing (that's more alliteration) moves in charismatic circles to "dumb down" the use of tongues.

I'm a tongue talker; I don't apologize. I think if there is something lacking, if we're not seeing something break through in the church setting or our private lives, it often stems from a downplaying of the importance of individuals, corporately and privately, praying in tongues. I've talked about the "fresh oil" of praying in tongues in my other books, the "building ourselves up" to keep in the love of God.

> *But you, beloved, building yourselves up on your most holy faith,*
> *praying in the Holy Spirit, keep yourselves in the love of God,*
> *looking for the mercy of our Lord Jesus Christ unto eternal life*
> (Jude 20-21).

But those same people should also know I endeavor to be a man of God's Word, through and through. I love God's Word; I attempt in all facets of my life, publicly and privately, to give it paramount significance.

One of the primary ways (not the *only* way, as we're attempting to show in this book) the Spirit intercedes through us is by speaking in tongues. But I also want to point out that it is the tongues in unison (working in tandem) with the Word—the Bible—being breathed on (*rhema* and *phero*; Strong's #4487 and #5342, if you're unfamiliar with those two Greek words) by the Holy Spirit. It is the Word and the Spirit flowing together that shows the activity of the glorious Intruder working upon our lives.

> *You will also declare a thing, and it will be established for you; so light will shine on your ways* (Job 22:28).

The Word is of utmost importance in all matters pertaining to releasing the fame of Jesus through the Spirit. Also, *our* words are important, when they are in line with *the* Word. What gives us the authority, the *boldness*, to speak and release heavenly things into earthly situations? The Word that is breathed on by the Spirit.

Remember He sent His Word and healed the people (see Ps. 107:20), and the people were astonished at the *authority* behind His words (again, Mark 1:27). In our effort not only to imitate Christ but manifest Him, we cannot overlook the importance of the Word and the Spirit, for *"Jesus answered and said unto them, Ye do err, not knowing the scriptures, nor the power of God"* (Matt. 22:29 KJV).

> *This Book of the Law shall not depart from your mouth, but you shall meditate in it day and night, that you may observe to do according to all that is written in it. For then you will make your way prosperous, and then you will have good success* (Joshua 1:8).

We are wise to live in the Word, and speak in the Spirit. Continually, constantly, without ceasing. To meditate on it, chew it over and over, but also blend it with our prayer life; that is, while speaking in tongues.

It's an interesting point to make about the "cloven tongues" of Acts 2:3 (KJV). "Cloven," or riven, is simply an archaic way of saying "split or divided in two"—or "twain" if you wanna get real old school about it. In the Old Testament, a "clean" animal was one with cloven hooves, chewing the cud (see Lev. 11). I'm not here to encourage living under the Law, but rather to point out the types and foreshadowing of it. The Lord demands a clean sacrifice when we worship and meditate on Him. It should be directed by His Spirit, and split into *two parts*: the Word and the Spirit. Cloven, two parts, splitting from a whole (thus blending together as one act of worship), while we are chewing our cuds. Did I drive the cow metaphor home well enough?

Our brains are separated into two halves: the right and the left hemispheres. The left being the realm of logic, the right being the realm of creativity: *"What is the conclusion then? I will pray with the spirit, and I will also pray with the understanding. I will sing with the spirit, and I will also sing with the understanding"* (1 Cor. 14:15). Again, two parts. The understanding (left-side process) and in the Spirit (right-side process). Look at it this way, praying in tongues releases your creative side!

"Sanctify them by Your truth. Your word is truth" (John 17:17). We are made clean through the washing of the water of the Word (see Eph. 5:26). We are set apart ("sanctified") by the Word. We throw off the imposed limitations of *fleshly living* so we can serve the Lord in Spirit and in truth (see John 4:24). Again, two parts flowing as one: Spirit and truth.

For added clarity on the cleanliness of our worship (which is to be a walk of life, a constant attitude), we could delineate "fleshly living" (dirty and unclean) according to the definition in Galatians 5 (verses 19-21) juxtaposed to the fresh, unsoiled fruit of the Spirit (verses 22-23). Fleshly living is the epitome of living under doctrines of legalism—read Galatians 5 in its context of the Law versus the freedom of the Spirit. We must walk cleanly in the Spirit.

TONGUES AND THE WORD

Tongues operating alongside the Word is important! After a fashion, it is the *lingua franca* of the kingdom—a significant means by which the Spirit communicates both *revelation and faith*. You probably know that *phero* means "rushing" in Acts 2:2, and it's the same word "moved" in Second Peter 1:21. I've talked at length about this maternity term in *Dancing Hand*, so I won't repeat myself here. But this *phero* is an aggressive act of the Holy Spirit, figuratively to be "born along by His breath," that which is the breath of first life—the shock of a baby's first inhalation. This activity of the Spirit is for the purpose of bringing forth *spiritual giants* in the breath of God. Our spirit-person must be activated, breathed on—this is *phero*. I've met many people who want to be spiritual giants in the faith, but they don't want to exercise their spirit to get to that point.

They are intimidated by the "breathing" of the Holy Ghost. But we need to be "moved" on by the Intruder—being overwhelmed by the Spirit brings the further revelation, the illumination of the Word, enlightening the eyes of our understanding (see Eph. 1:18), making intercession for us so that *"all things work together for good"* (see Rom. 8:27-28). See, in that passage, it is that which has been *breathed on by the Spirit*—it is in the context of His intercession through us that all things work together for good. That which is revealed and illuminated (we could say *rhema* that is *phero*'d) by Him—remember, **faith only operates when there is revelation**. As we pray in tongues, through the Holy Spirit's help, we can actually begin to *believe* what we are in need of *right out of our spirits*. It is given action by the Spirit's moving, and we can "declare a thing" and watch it be established. Indeed, light will shine on our way as the glory is released, backing up our proclamations. These are the "mysteries" we are speaking when we pray in tongues. Things to be revealed. It is for self-edification, building ourselves up!

> *For he who speaks in a tongue does not speak to men but to God, for no one understands him; however, in the spirit he speaks mysteries. But he who prophesies speaks edification and exhortation and comfort to men. He who speaks in a tongue edifies himself, but he who prophesies edifies the church* (1 Corinthians 14:2-4).

It's been taught by many theologians that there are *seven "levels" of tongues.* I get asked about these all the time, so hang in there, we'll cover them all. And remember, no one level is "better" than another or more important; they are numbered to show differentiation and certain times of usage.

The first level of tongues, one of the initial signs of evidence in the baptism of the Holy Spirit, is **our heavenly prayer language**, which sets the stage for this kind of activity of faith working through revelation that we just talked about. It certainly did work for the early Church in Acts 2. It was in their devotions and worship (see Acts 2:11—they were "speaking in our own tongues the *wonderful works of God...")* that they were birthed (*phero*'d) in a deeper revelation of the Spirit's aggressive activity.

For what was the product of their cloven tongues?

BOLDNESS

> *And when they had prayed, the place where they were assembled together was shaken; and they were all filled with the Holy Spirit, and they spoke the word of God with boldness* (Acts 4:31).

You probably know "boldness" is the Greek *parresia* (Strong's #3954, pronounced "par-ray-see-uh"). It means "to pour forth all," to speak unreservedly, to have the freedom to speak openly, frankly, clearly, without mincing words. The term conveys "freedom; fearless confidence; cheerful courage; assurance." And note this: "the deportment (that means 'demeanor, posture, manner, behavior') by which one becomes conspicuous or secures publicity." Modernized, that means "the way we carry ourselves that spreads fame." The means by which the Spirit, through our boldness, because of His boldness, spreads the fame of Jesus Christ. It attracts the attention of the public. All from releasing our heavenly tongues!

By exercising our spirits praying in tongues, it synergizes us with the Holy Spirit. Check out the Amplified version for First Corinthians 14:14: *"For if I pray in an [unknown] tongue, my spirit [by the Holy Spirit within me] prays, but my mind is unproductive [it bears no fruit and helps nobody]."* That's the concept: *my* spirit by *the* Spirit within me. Synergism. It is the mechanism by which the Spirit works with us to build our lives; that which was laid to ruin (mentally, emotionally, physically, spiritually) is restored (lifted up). We could say when you pray in tongues, you build your spiritual home. The mind itself does not comprehend this work (i.e., praying in tongues sounds like gibberish); therefore, to your brain, it is unproductive. But while not understanding it, even our minds are lifted up beyond the natural when we speak in tongues.

I've said it before, but it bears repeating: in Acts 2:11 and Luke 1:49, both "wonderful works" and "great things" is *megaleios* (Strong's #3167, "may-ga-lie-oss") in the Greek; the only two such occurrences of the word in the New Testament. The context of "wonderful works" is after the infilling of the Holy Spirit, speaking in tongues the greatness of God; "great things" is Mary's Song, the Magnificat, hailing the coming birth of the Messiah.

The connection? Speaking in tongues, bearing the Messiah.

When we speak in tongues, we bear the works of the Messiah into every situation and area of need. He does "wonderful works" and "great things" as Christ the Anointed One—His anointing comes and penetrates, surrounds, enlarges, and overwhelms the circumstances. The Spirit works through us to *megaleios* the mighty One whose name is holy.

Here's another word study freebie; you're welcome, I did the work for you. Romans 8:26, "groanings" is *stenagmos* (Strong's #4726, "stay-nog-moss"), which comes from *stenazo* (Strong's #4727, "stay-nah-zoh")—"to sigh" as in Mark 7:34.

Go ahead, sigh with me.

Now here's where it gets interesting. This word comes from *stenos* (Strong's #4728, "stay-noss"), an adjective meaning "narrow, strait." To be placed or set firmly. As in the "strait gate" of Matthew 7:13 and Luke 13:24. Strait means to be placed in a narrow, confined space with very little room (uh, like a straitjacket), a difficult situation involving hardship. We pray nearly inaudibly, unintelligibly ("cannot be uttered"); we can't express it in words, so we groan. Thus, we sigh because there isn't much room to breathe. *"We ourselves groan within ourselves."* (Rom. 8:23, *stenazo*). We exhale to get some wiggle room. Likewise, the Spirit groans within us.

For what purpose? These groanings bring our mind, emotions, and bodies in line with the Spirit's work, overcoming the infirmity of the flesh. Groanings bring deliverance from within and push back the pressures of darkness from without. Indeed, arise and shine!

Groanings push us into the *zoe* life, through the "tight places," those places of distress that seem to bind us, into the larger places of the Spirit. Groanings move deep within us and cause us to become open and vulnerable to the Spirit, so that He works through us, bringing us into a bright place that we might spread the fame of Christ to others. Groanings prepare us for the utter abandonment that God requires of His sons.

Those who are self-satisfied will have great difficulty in groaning with the Spirit, and those who are *desperate* will have difficulty in *not* groaning with the Spirit!

Because I said we'd talk about the various levels of tongues, let's move on to another level: **the gift of tongues** that's mentioned in First Corinthians 12:10, "*...to another different kinds of tongues, to another the interpretation of tongues.*" The original King James says "*divers kinds of tongues.*" Not deep-sea divers, but diverse. These are tongues in the public assembly. These are the tongues Paul is addressing in the following verses: "*And God hath set some in the church...diversities of tongues...do all speak with tongues? do all interpret?*" (1 Cor. 12:28,30 KJV).

This passage is in the context of gifts of the Spirit to the Body. (He's talking about apostles, prophets, gifts of healings, helps, governments—the ways of the Spirit among the church body.) Those opposed to a personal baptism of the Holy Spirit with the evidence of speaking in tongues cite this passage as confirmation against a personal prayer language being available to all born-again Christians; but of course, deeper study of Paul's statements (see 1 Cor. 14:5,18 for further example) outline his desire that all saints would be open to the personal intercession of the Holy Spirit (as well as the release of this second type of tongues in the public setting, when appropriate and when interpreted for the whole church's understanding).

But for this second type of tongues, a gift in the public setting, "divers" (again, not the scuba kind) could carry a connotation of great joy and festivity, similar to "diversities of gifts" in verse 4 of chapter 12. The tongues and interpretation represent a *celebration* with God; dare I say a "party" with God in tongues? Hence the expression "intoxicated in the Spirit." For there is an element of cathartic release, and an atmosphere of elation, rapture, merriment, and giddiness associated with this type of manifestation of the Spirit.

Tongues and interpretation of those tongues define what the Spirit is doing among the congregation, an imprint of Himself and His current expression at that moment—in other words, these gifts are used to release the expression of God to the people, the marked imprint of God's grace and favor upon His children, stirring up an excitement and exuberant outburst of "par-tay!" Which is why they are a sign to the unbeliever (see 1 Cor. 14:22).

Let's not forget the early Church was born with the sign of intoxication! The people from other nations were attracted by what they *heard* and what they saw, assuming they were drunk. And after a fashion, they were; I mean, the Christians were completely abandoned to God, celebrating, merrymaking.

> *I am like a drunken man, and like a man whom wine has overcome, because of the Lord, and because of His holy words* (Jeremiah 23:9).

Here was Jeremiah prophesying to a people group under the bondage of the Babylonian system. It was like he was dealing with the judgmental spirits that pervaded the Israelites; he was breaking the mindsets created by false prophets who loved the status quo.

Look at it this way, the anointing of drunkenness (that'll preach!) is offensive to the principalities and powers that cause the Church to be lukewarm. *The power is in the offense that tongues create.*

Just one more way the glorious Intruder helps overcome our infirmities. And indeed, what better way to spread the fame of Jesus Christ than with a celebration of the miraculous, drunk in the Holy Ghost, speaking with His divers tongues. Dive right on in, the water's fine!

So is the new wine! It's potent, intimate with the Spirit—it reminds me of the high priest's garments in Exodus. Follow me here for a second.

> *You shall make the robe of the ephod all of blue* (Exodus 28:31).

Blue. The color of heavenly places, right? With the little golden bells, and the pomegranates (see Exod. 28, 39, et al.). Then three colors in Exodus 28:33: blue, purple, scarlet.

The pomegranate fruit is indigenous to Iran. It's been used for millennia to represent prosperity (because it has so many seeds). Like clustered grapes, pomegranates can be made into a strong drink, and the juice is used in grenadine. Even in modern times, the intoxicating properties (and medicinal as well) of pomegranates are becoming more and more widespread in Western civilization. (I'm not advocating rushing out and buying a bottle of pomegranate booze—I'm talking about the metaphoric properties here, the foreshadows and representations.)

We know the gold bells represent the glory of God, the striking of the bell symbolizing the release of that divine unction—the tangible presence of God, like sweet, tinkling music to the ears.

The blue of the pomegranates, we've discussed—the heavenlies. Purple, the color of royalty. Scarlet, obviously the redemptive power of innocent blood shed for the sins of another.

Is it too much of a stretch to think perhaps the high priest was "intoxicated" as he entered the holy of holies? They were worried about him being killed by the overpowering glory of God, hence the bells making noise—he must still be alive in there! Obviously there would be some kind of physical reaction! Moses was not able to enter the tabernacle because of the glory (see Exod. 40:35).

Another facet of tongues is used as a weapon. That may be an odd thought, I know. Praying in tongues as a weapon.

> And do not present your members as instruments of unrighteousness to sin, but present yourselves to God as being alive from the dead, and your members as instruments of righteousness to God (Romans 6:13).

That word "instruments" is hoplon (Strong's #3696, "ha-plon") and it means "tools, implements, arms, weapons of warfare." Our members, including our tongues, are to be yielded to the Intruder as weapons of righteousness. As we travail in tongues, the Spirit is working through us powerful armaments that tear down strongholds. We stand in the gap and wage warfare through tongues.

> *For with stammering lips and another tongue He will speak to this people, to whom He said, "This is the rest with which you may cause the weary to rest," and, "This is the refreshing"; yet they would not hear* (Isaiah 28:11-12).

We're talking about tongues as a Holy Spirit expression of our depth of desire, our passion, being supercharged by divine energy, thus being fashioned as a missile that tears down devilish activity. These kinds of warfare tongues are filled with boldness and filled with burden that the Spirit places within us. A spiritual hunger to stand in the gap and intercede. Again, it is rest in the midst of activity—an aggressive, overwhelming work of the Intruder.

That rest Isaiah was prophesying is similar to the rest in Hebrews 4. Verses 8 and 9 of that chapter talk about two different kinds of rest (they're different Greek words). One is the final rest, the all-Sabbath rest, the reward for Christians—that's still remaining. Our blessed eternal reward. The other is rest from weariness and warring attacks, summed up in the Hebrew word "Noah" as in the ark "resting" from its battle with the waters. *Selah.*

In Greek, this is *katapauo* (Strong's #2664, *kah-tah-pow-oh*), sometimes transliterated *catapausis*. Do you see a similar English word somewhere in there?

Catapult. A weapon of throwing down.

The "rest" is a causing to cease, a putting down of, disposing of power (stopping function), casting down your enemies. Anything that tries to dominate and weaken the fiber of your spirit. These are tongues of deliverance, giving His people a language of deliverance. This is war, and rest in war. This is the glorious Intruder spreading the fame of Jesus Christ through you.

> *Raise a song and strike the timbrel, the pleasant harp with the lute. Blow the trumpet at the time of the New Moon, at the full moon, on our solemn feast day. For this is a statute for Israel, a law of the God of Jacob. This He established in Joseph as a testimony, when He went throughout the land of Egypt, where I heard a language I did not understand* (Psalm 81:2-5).

You can shout if you want to.

What other types of tongues are there?

> *Then He said to His disciples, "The harvest truly is plentiful, but the laborers are few. Therefore pray the Lord of the harvest to send out laborers into His harvest"* (Matthew 9:37-38).

Tongues can be used to bring in the lost. We've already talked about tongues being a sign to the unbelievers (see 1 Cor. 14:22-25), and that tongues are a form of intercession and divine intervention into the way the earth system currently works. This level of tongues in intercession may be accompanied by a face brought before you—someone who is lost—you intercede for this person, and they are birthed into the kingdom, the harvest is brought in.

The sign of tongues is an affront to the unbelieving. For the Church in Paul's time, it was a sign to the Gnostics that they were not where they should have been spiritually. All supernatural activity has a confrontational aspect to its release. People must decide, "Either you're all crazy, or God is in this place." One or the other. *"For the message of the cross is foolishness to those who are perishing, but to us who are being saved it is the power of God"* (1 Cor. 1:18). The power of God is revealed through the release of tongues, not giving way to bedlam with the whole church in a confusing barrage of "shabbahs" and "shondais," but everything being done decently and in order (and yet still, *all things* being done; see 1 Cor. 14:40); the Lord uses the sign of tongues as just another way to arrest the attention of the harvest.

Those brought into captivity must speak captive language. So this type of tongues can also be a sign of judgment to the "unbelieving" believers, you know?

> *O earth, earth, earth, hear the word of the Lord! Thus says the Lord: "Write this man down as childless, a man who shall not prosper in his days; for none of his descendants shall prosper, sitting on the throne of David, and ruling anymore in Judah"* (Jeremiah 22:29-30).

Let's not leave ourselves childless, let us gather the harvest, let us birth people into the kingdom through this travail, let us press into the release of tongues so the Intruder may crash upon our communities and neighborhoods, affecting change. Indeed, these types of tongues are a sign of salvation to the unsaved.

As First Corinthians 14 shows, tongues move into releasing the gift of prophecy for evangelism. The thoughts and intents of the disbelieving heart are revealed. We cannot neglect the importance of tongues in spreading the fame of Christ.

One of the levels that everyone gives a small smile about is tongues released during crisis situations, these **tongues of emergency.** People smile because nearly all of us have been there before, even though the situations requiring this type of tongues are *not* funny. "Lord Jesus, help! Now!" You burst into these tongues as you see the makings of a car wreck before you, and somehow the Lord protects, the car swerves, and you exhale. "Thank You, Lord!"

And when the Lord intervenes, we look back on that situation, saying, "Whew, Lord, if You hadn't've jumped in *right then*...I don't know what I would've done." This type of tongues is pleading for

God's mercy and intervention, tongues of supplication for divine protection.

There are tongues that are released as the **language of the kingdom of God**. Declarations.

> *God is not a man, that He should lie, nor a son of man, that He should repent. Has He said, and will He not do? Or has He spoken, and will He not make it good? Behold, I have received a command to bless; He has blessed, and I cannot reverse it. He has not observed iniquity in Jacob, nor has He seen wickedness in Israel. The Lord his God is with him, and **the shout of a King is among them**. God brings them out of Egypt; He has strength like a wild ox. For there is no sorcery against Jacob, nor any divination against Israel. It now must be said of Jacob and of Israel, "Oh, what God has done!" Look, a people rises like a lioness, and lifts itself up like a lion; it shall not lie down until it devours the prey, and drinks the blood of the slain* (Numbers 23:19-24).

The shout of the King is among them! To rule, and to reign, to further the kingdom, to roar as a lion. Every satanic device is turned back, every curse turned to a blessing. This type of tongues is a proclamation of blessing, the SHOUT! This includes holy laughter, extravagant praise, these types of expressions coupled with the tongues of the kingdom.

You can shout again if you want to, I won't tell.

Perhaps the most important type of tongues release, at least pertaining to the release of the aggressive intervention of the Intruder, is the **tongues of the Father Himself**. What I mean by this is, we get to a place in our prayer life where we sit silently, rapt, mute, and He speaks to us in His own words, His own language; we just listen. This level of tongues is only found in the secret place, and we need the help of the Holy Spirit, the Paraclete, One called alongside, an expert in His field, giving aid to us, the needy. It is only as we allow Him—by yielding our lives and tongues, our emotions, our wills, our spirits—that we are placed in a position to hear the Father's voice speak to us in this fashion. The barriers around our spirit-person are torn down, and we become overwhelmed by the encounter. It is *ekstasis.*

In First Kings 19, Elijah experienced an ecstatic encounter with the tongues of the Father in the "still, small voice" (verse 12). The Hebrew word that is translated "still" is *demamah* (Strong's #1827, "dem-ah-mah") and comes from a primitive root implying shocked into silence, astounded, to be dumbstruck. It is also closely related to a root meaning to wash, purge, cleanse, cast out.

The word "small" is *daq* (Strong's #1851, "dack"), and it comes from a primitive root meaning to pulverize, to crush, literally "make dust." It is also closely related to a root meaning to tread down or trample.

So while "still, small voice" sounds kind of wimpy in modern English, we can actually see it is an extremely powerful voice that has the ability to astonish, crush, and cleanse. When we encounter this still, small voice, we are astonished, dumbfounded, overwhelmed to the point of silence. Being unable to even articulate in our language. Muted in rapturous awe.

The only sounds that can escape our lips are "groanings which cannot be uttered"—revelation of the power of God that overcomes us to the point our tongues don't work right, so all we can do is go, "Mmmm. Uhhhh. Ahhhh. Oooohhh. Ohhhh."

This is what struck Elijah when confronted with the still, small voice—a rapturous, euphoric experience.

So by my count, that's the seven types of tongues. If you have not been released in a heavenly prayer language, or even think perhaps it's "evil" or a "sign of past times, not for today," please let me do my absolute best to assure you that is not the case.

Yes, if you are saved, you have the Holy Spirit living inside you—that is a condition of the born-again experience, God Himself residing within your spirit; hence, everlasting life in His presence. The Holy Spirit baptizes you into Christ at the moment of your conversion. You have the Holy Spirit. The question is, "Does He have all of you?" You've probably heard the illustration from tongue-talkers before. When you're saved, the Holy Spirit is as a cupful, a never-ending cupful to be sure, but your own personal well of Water: *"But whoever drinks of the water that I shall give him will never thirst. But the water that I shall give him will become in him a fountain of water springing up into everlasting life"* (John 4:14).

Being filled with the Spirit, subsequent to your salvation experience, is that same cup overflowing, being dropped in the ocean: *"On the last day, that great day of the feast, Jesus stood and cried out, saying, 'If anyone thirsts, let him come to Me and drink. He who believes in Me, as the Scripture has said, out of his heart will **flow rivers of living water**.' But this He spoke concerning the Spirit, whom those believing in Him would receive; for the Holy Spirit was not yet given, because Jesus was not yet glorified"* (John 7:37-39).

It is more Water than you know what to do with, so in turn, you give it away to others. (This is the "spreading the fame of Jesus" part. The anointing of the Holy Spirit flowing forth as a river, unstoppable, never flagging.)

The gift of the Holy Spirit is the promise of the Father. (Again John 14:16, *"And I will pray the Father, and He will give you another Helper, that He may abide with you forever…."*)

"And when He had said this, He breathed on them, and said to them, 'Receive the Holy Spirit.'" *(John 20:22).* It was at this moment the Spirit began to reside within the disciples—they became born again. But note there was a subsequent baptism in the Holy Spirit in Acts 2.

> *Then Peter said to them, "Repent, and let every one of you be baptized in the name of Jesus Christ for the remission of sins; and you shall receive the gift of the Holy Spirit. For the promise is to*

you and to your children, and to all who are afar off, as many as the Lord our God will call" (Acts 2:38-39).

Look, dear reader, we cannot neglect the importance of tongues in all levels in our lives. This whole book has been about the aggressive help of the Holy Spirit—one of the primary ways He executes this help is through the release of our heavenly language. Don't downplay such a powerful weapon in our arsenal!

Perhaps here's a good place to share some illustrations of the help of the Holy Spirit, and specifically the release of warfare, emergency tongues. Let me turn the keyboard over to my lovely wife, Joy, and let her share these testimonies in her own words. Pay attention, when Joy speaks, people would do well to listen!

5

JOY

I HAVE COME FAIRLY CLOSE TO DEATH ON THREE OCCASIONS, ALL stemming from unrelated issues arising between the summer of 1976 and the summer of 1978. In those two short years, my husband's faith would be strongly tested. I say *his* faith, because these incidences all arose quickly and seemingly out of nowhere. In all three situations I found myself being thrown from a routine day into a crucial life-or-death confrontation. Therefore, finding myself suddenly caught off-guard in a virtual riptide of the quest for survival, I daresay my fate came to rest upon my husband's response in moments of surprise crisis. As for me, well, I was fairly distracted with the battle itself.

I am fully persuaded that had not my husband stood his ground in faith, refusing to relinquish me to the next world, I most certainly would be there now! I am very much anticipating my graduation to heaven after a lifetime of serving the Lord here below. But I am convinced the devil takes advantage in many circumstances and tries to thwart the purposes of God wherever he can slip in a foothold. Many fine, unsuspecting Christians have been unprepared for such sudden challenges. I imagine most believers would not respond the same way my husband did when the enemy attempted to subvert God's plan for my life.

People may take issue with me as to whether the devil could really succeed in cutting a Christian's life short. It is much more comforting to assume he could never do so. I personally believe he has attacked many unsuspecting souls who were not ready for such. I, myself, was greatly in love with the Lord at the time, but I was by no means a giant in faith. On my own, I do believe my life would have been cut short. The Lord would have welcomed me into His heaven, but the timing was premature. It wasn't time for me to graduate because I had not yet fulfilled my calling on this planet.

We all pray to be found in the center of God's will. I feel I would have missed out on His best plan had I departed this world early. We all know the Lord can take what the devil meant for harm, and turn it around for His glory (see Ps. 21; Gen. 50:19-21). God uses these high-pressure experiences as a proving ground to develop bedrock faith in us.

No child of God can survive without trust. And most of us have that base covered. One cannot attend too many church services without hearing sermons about trust! We learn early on that childlike trust in our Father's providential care is the foundation of the peace we experience in Him. We become persuaded that neither life nor death can separate us from the love of God (see Rom. 8:38-39)—and most certainly neither can.

However, few of us press beyond the basic element of trust in the Lord. As truly as hope is our anchor (see Heb. 6:19) and trust is our foundation, there remains yet another element: that of faith. All are necessary. However, we seem to hear more messages about hope and trust than we do about faith.

Trust is vital. Trust is passive. Trust rests as the babe in the Father's arms. It is irreplaceable in the child's relationship with the Lord. In addition, though often neglected—but just as vital—exists faith. What is the difference between trust and faith? Faith is active rather than passive. If trust were a state-of-being verb, as "being at rest," then faith is an action verb! Trust *rests*, but faith *does*. Trust is necessary as our platform. But we shouldn't just stop there. *Trust* needs to become the springboard from which *faith* launches into action. These two work together, one recessive and one dominant, one receiving and the other acting. This is the work of the Holy Spirit, as we yield to His help and work alongside Him in developing our lives in Christ.

Trust sails us through the daily ups and downs of our lives. The Amplified Bible shows that when we believe *(pisteuo,* Strong's #4100, "pis-to-oh"—to cleave, to adhere), we are relying upon and clinging to the Lord. We "stick like glue" to Him. We are dependent upon Him. That's trust. We'll never make it to the other side without trust!

Suddenly, on the horizon may approach an ominous dark cloud, threatening to wipe out our small boat! This is the time for action! This is the time for faith.

I was minding my own business one lovely Saturday morning in June. We were planning to drive a couple of hours away to minister Sunday morning. I was about to get up and start my day, but…I couldn't get up! Some burning knife had pierced my abdomen, it seemed. Could I maybe move, or perhaps sit up? No. I'd never been shot with a gun, but I pictured I had taken a searing bullet to my left lower abdomen.

My husband began to wonder why I couldn't get up, and when I told him the problem, he prayed over me as any good husband should. The pain did not abate, so he retreated to our "prayer closet," (the bathroom of our little apartment), to "storm heaven," as we used to term it in the olden days!

Every time he came out to check on me, the pain level was still severe. This went on into the afternoon. Finally, as he returned yet again to the prayer closet, he heard an audible instruction from the Spirit, "Take Joy to the hospital or she will die." That was a strange thing to hear, but he promptly obeyed. Lifting me out of bed (thank goodness I only weighed 97 pounds at the time), he carried me to the car and drove me to the hospital just five minutes away.

In the emergency room, I waited seven hours to see a doctor. Apparently downtown Dallas had many people in the throes of death, and I would have to wait my turn. Numerous interns approached from time to time, pushing on my belly, noting that it was swelling up. I will never forget one query put to me, "Is everything okay at home and at work? Might you be going through relationship struggles or work pressure?" Through my gritted teeth I answered, "Everything is great, except this stabbing pain in my abdomen that is very real."

Finally, a sweet nurse said they needed to stick a syringe into my abdomen to see if I might perhaps be bleeding internally. It was very curious how my flat stomach had now swollen to mimic the size of a pregnancy. A huge vial that looked something like what a veterinarian might use on a horse was presented. The nurse offered her hand for me to squeeze and told me to lie very still. She said I could concentrate my entire reaction to the pain onto her hand—not to worry about hurting her—just squeeze as hard as I needed! When I saw the tube quickly fill with dark blood, I watched her eyes grow wide. I also felt ashamed that my fingernails had dug bloody gouges into her pretty hand.

Then the room grew very dark, and I wondered why they lowered the lights. I also was trembling with cold so that my teeth rattled. They began to bring hot blankets straight from the dryer to place on me. Oh, how very wonderful they felt! I looked at my husband whose face seemed to be getting smaller. I watched as they told him they surmised I must have had a tubal pregnancy, unknown to me, and it probably burst the fallopian tube causing all the internal bleeding.

I was too out of it to exercise faith. I was utterly reliant upon my husband to stand in faith for me! I managed to say, "If you're a man of God, I'll come through this thing, but if not—it's on *your* shoulders."

Jim had been keeping vigil those seven hours, and all he had with him was a little pocket New Testament. Being a prophet, he has always been prone to seeing and hearing things in the spirit realm that I am quite happy *not* to know about! He saw demons attacking me, horrid imps that sneered into his face, shaking their fists at him, laughing and saying, "We've got her now! She's dead, and your life's over, your ministry's thwarted! She's ours!"

They were proud to be cutting me off, and happy to see him lose his bride of one year.

Tears dripped onto the little New Testament when all of a sudden First Peter 1:5 jumped off the page, *"who are **kept** by the power of God through faith for salvation ready to be revealed in the last time."* This word "kept" is the Greek word *phroureo* (Strong's #5432, "froo-ray-oh," meaning "before/above, to perceive, behold, take heed"). It is a military term picturing a sentry standing guard as protection against the enemy: "To protect by a military guard, to prevent hostile invasion, to protect by guarding and watching, to preserve one for the attainment of something."

For seven hours my husband stood in the gap between life and death on my behalf. He stood with God to "keep" me. I was in too much pain to stand in faith, so he "made up the hedge" for me. For seven hours, he saw, smelled, and heard those hideous imps as they mocked him.

"We've got her now!" squealed in one ear, ever so loudly. "She's going to die!"

But a still, small Voice (see 1 Kings 19:11-12) whispered in the other ear, "She's going to live." It was barely able to be heard over the demonic tumult, but it was there.

"She's going to die!"

"She's going to live..." *Who are kept by the power of God through faith...*

Jim went out to the car and looked up to heaven to ask a word of the Lord for me. And the word came, "It isn't a tubal pregnancy. It is a very large growth that has exploded the ovary and fallopian tube, causing the hemorrhage."

He quickly left the parking lot and hurried inside to tell the interns what was wrong with me. At that moment, a wonderfully brilliant Jewish surgeon appeared at my side. After seven hours in the hands of bewildered interns, it was amazing to look into the knowing eyes of this specialist. He took one glance at me and said, "This is a ruptured ovary, and we have maybe ten minutes to save this woman's life."

The nurse quipped, "Why wasn't she seen sooner than this?"

He replied, "I've been saving lives all day long."

After four hours of suffering at home followed by seven hours in the emergency room, all I wanted was reprieve. Without the surgeon saying so, I already knew I was in the death process, as I was slipping away from my body. It seemed so much easier just to leave than to keep clinging to life by my fingernails. My breathing had grown so shallow as the blood filled my abdomen, pushing up under my lungs. There just wasn't any room left to breathe. I gasped for tiny bits of breath, but each one hurt too badly. I thought I would just leave.

But I didn't feel the presence of the Lord, so I knew He was not pleased with me leaving! It couldn't be His will for me to go, or else I would have felt Him near. In fact, I felt something very *un*godly around me.

My husband saw the death angel descend like a black cloud, hovering over me, and watched the light go out of my eyes as they rushed me to emergency surgery. I heard him rebuke the spirit of death as they zipped me through swinging doors.

He later told me the Lord spoke to him the moment the death angel descended. Even in the midst of this horrific experience, the Lord told Jim there was something to be learned here: "So that you may know you have power over even death itself, point your finger at the spirit and rebuke it in My name!"

So Jim did. He rebuked the spirit of death in the name of Jesus and it departed.

I heard the nurse ask, "What about prepping?"

And the smart surgeon shot back, "No time," as they ran, pushing the gurney.

It turned out I had lost half my body's blood supply, which is the point of death. The surgeon was very accurate on his timing, and God got him out of another surgery just in the nick of time to come save my life.

I learned that day that the devil can catch us off guard. You can wake up a healthy twenty-year-old and be dying that very day. I also learned that the power of God will *keep* us. But it's not always automatic. We are kept "through faith…." Faith is something that is grown from the size of a mustard seed to one of the largest bushes in the Middle Eastern flora. Faith comes by hearing, and hearing by the word of God (see Rom. 10:17). It is a work of the Holy Spirit, the growing of faith, as we work alongside Him.

Faith was the action on my husband's part that intervened on that pretty June day. And two weeks later we moved to Kentucky to begin full-time ministry as pastors. The devil wanted to defeat us before we even got started, but he didn't win.

So I lived! And I got to become a mother! The following June was spent throwing up, and I was so happy to be "in the family way" as the older women in Kentucky referred to my "condition." We had miscarried a baby before the ovarian rupture, and I had known women who had trouble getting pregnant with just one ovary. But by December, I had doubled my entire weight. (It was a good thing my husband didn't need to pick me up and carry me to the car!) Yes, I was truly "great with child" early in the Christmas month.

THEN...

Due to toxemia, the doctor decided I should be induced early rather than waiting until Christmas when the baby was due. (I suppose he had holiday plans that helped him make that decision!) I checked into our so-very-tiny hospital in our little, bitty town. I thought, *This hospital is smaller than the small-town nursing home where we used to sing songs on Sunday afternoon.*

There was no maternity ward in the one story building—I was across the hall from an elderly man. As soon as the young girl started the Pitocin drip in my IV, I knew she had done it wrong. (It seemed there was only one true nurse at any time on duty, being aided by a couple of candy-stripers.) I had read it should be a very slow rate of drip at first, but what I saw instead was a constant drip, one immediately following another. I told the young girl it had to be wrong, and sure enough, by the time she asked around and got it corrected quite a while later, I had gone from no labor whatsoever to transition-type contractions.

The very first contractions I experienced came every two minutes apart and lasted thirty seconds. In no way did it resemble natural labor. I knew I was being artificially propelled into contractions that were far too sudden and close together, so I never got to go through the normal stages of labor. But even when the Pitocin was regulated, the contractions could not slow down. I had read about the stress this would put on the baby, causing constriction during each contraction without enough time between for the baby to recover. But this tiny hospital didn't have modern monitors like the big cities had. All the nurse had was a stethoscope! And there was nothing that could be done.

Although the labor was only ten hours long, which is not an undue length for a first delivery, the contractions were not appropriate. There was no proper rest time between contractions, and no time to gradually build up. I couldn't believe what I was timing now: contractions lasting two minutes long, with only a thirty second break before the next one came! But there was still a lot of dilation needed.

I began completely passing out for those thirty seconds in between each contraction, losing consciousness each time. It seemed the dilation quit progressing at eight centimeters, and we had come to a standstill. Finally the doctor said we could wait no longer, and I was wheeled to the delivery room.

The doctor began at four A.M. trying to deliver with forceps. He pulled on the baby's head so forcibly that I was pulled clear off the delivery table and landed on the floor! I was never so shocked in my entire life to find myself on that hard tile floor! He was upset and visibly shaken by now, so he stationed a girl at each armpit, yelling orders for them to hold me up on the table while he pulled.

By now I had a mental image of how some ranchers in Texas help the mother cows. They wrap a chain around the calf's ankles and attach the other end to their pick-up truck, and then start backing up!

He pulled for one hour, another statistic that made me wish I didn't read so much. I knew what that could do to a baby, and that being stuck in the birth canal for an hour was like a death sentence. I personally knew a woman back in Texas whose doctor had pulled too much and severed the nerves in the baby's neck and shoulder. That child's arm hung useless at his side his entire life.

And I thought of far worse things—the brain damage this would cause!

Finally at five A.M. my baby was born, "sunny side up" rather than facing downward. He was nearly eight pounds and had strong lungs and good color. (But I thought, *What's up with that red hair? Where did **that** come from?*)

The momentary rejoicing quickly gave way to grave panic. I looked at the sheer horror on my doctor's face as blood spurted from my body all over his clothes. It was as though someone had turned on the garden hose and was shooting blood up into the air. Not to be too graphic here, but something had been ripped out.

The doctor screamed, *"Get the father out of here!"* The two girls started trying to push him out of the door. Jim commenced praying out loudly in warfare, emergency tongues. As they shoved him out the door, he shouted, *"In the name of Jesus—I rebuke you, death! I rebuke the flow of blood!"*

The doctor looked like he wished someone were pushing *him* out the door. It's hard to have confidence when you see your doctor turning white, with his mouth gaping open in shock, and the spray of your own blood drenching him.

I thought, *Well, I didn't die last year, but here I go now. But it was worth it, bringing this little guy into the world. That's what matters.* I understood the old saying that a mother will go to the gates of death for her child.

As they were pushing Jim out the door and he was rebuking the flow of blood, the doctor yelled, *"My God, my God! I'm witnessing a miracle here!"* My husband watched the doctor yell in shock as an organ-looking thing went back inside the birth canal. I don't mean to be too explicit here, but I'm just sharing what happened. Jim told me later that some blood actually went in reverse, back inside me. Unseen hands were putting things back in place.

And then, just as suddenly as the spraying had started, it stopped. Just like that. Nothing. The doctor just stood there trembling and weak-kneed, and I wondered if he'd lost control of his bodily functions. I felt so sorry for the poor young girls who didn't look like they could be nurses yet. (Who knows if that experience made them lose interest in a medical career.)

I was wheeled to my room, and an older nurse was stationed beside my bed for twelve hours, followed by another nurse for twelve more hours. I also felt sorry for them because that chair didn't look at all comfortable all those hours. Their job was to monitor my vitals every fifteen minutes for the first twenty-four hours.

Because I had lost so much blood, I required transfusions, five units worth. I thought, *Here we go again, getting all this new blood when I was just getting used to the other peoples' blood I got last year.*

After five days of observation, I was released to go home. And wouldn't you know it, the baby, Andrew, was normal! Or better than normal. He weighed fifteen pounds at his seven week check-up and twenty pounds at his three month check-up! Brain damage? No. He was very smart instead. (My mom was a little concerned about the severely sloped forehead caused by the hard birth, but he ended up a handsome lad.)

I realize people in the medical profession will say I don't have my facts straight, that this story is impossible and doesn't line up with any sort of sense whatsoever. I know I risk sounding delusional, and I know I'm not savvy enough to explain it in medical terms. So I'm just telling you what happened because I had a front row seat. All I know is the Lord fixed something very wrong just in the nick of time. And how to explain the protection for my baby during that crazy labor, much less the crazier birth? Once again, my husband had stood in faith for me at a time when I didn't feel I could make the stand. The Holy Spirit was working alongside Jim to push him into standing in the gap for me.

When I saw the doctor for my follow-up visit, he had regained all his composure and just talked about what a "fine specimen of a male child" I had. As I was about to leave the room, he got a very serious look on his face and said, "I've delivered 670 babies, but I never witnessed anything like that in my life. I'd advise you to *never* have another child."

Then he looked into my eyes and, with a reverential tone in his voice, said, "It was a miracle, what happened that night. Only God could do what I saw happen in front of my eyes." I said, "You're so right about that, Doctor."

And once again I knew how blessed I was to have Jesus so involved in our lives. I called Him "The God Who Intervenes." He certainly was doing that on a regular basis, up close and personal.

But I figured from now on, maybe we wouldn't need so much last-minute intervention. That spur of the moment, life-or-death thing was awesome, but very overwhelming. Surely I'd had my fair share.

AND THEN...

When baby Andrew was almost nine months old, I had some oral surgery done. Everything went well, and the doctor sent me home with a prescription for pain medication. We were staying at my parents' house, and a revival was going on at our home church. So I told my husband to go on to the meeting that night because I had my mom to watch Andrew and take care of anything I might need.

I was resting on the bed in the back den and got up to go to the adjacent bathroom. Something suddenly was terribly wrong. My chest clenched up tight, and I fell down onto the floor while trying to get back to the bed. I simply could not get up and was in excruciating pain so that I could barely catch a breath. I thought, *I can't even call out to Mama.*

Just about then, my mom came through the kitchen, which opened to the den where I was lying. She glanced down with an expression of trying to assess and register the situation. At that moment, I heard the front door open and my husband returning. Mom quickly headed toward the front room, and I could hear her trying to talk to him about Joy being white as a sheet, but he never stopped to listen. She later told me that as soon as he flung the front door open, he hurriedly walked right past her straight back to the den, like a man on a mission.

He already knew my condition, for the Lord had shown him before he came inside the house.

As he brushed by my mom, without hesitation he lifted me up onto the bed. It felt as though an elephant were sitting on my chest; and to make matters worse, now my husband stretched himself on top of me! But then I realized he was doing exactly what Elijah did when he stretched himself out on the dead boy (see 1 Kings 17:21). As he prayed in the Spirit and commanded death to lift off me, I began to feel an intense heat in my chest. It felt like when you have a Charlie horse or muscle spasm that's tied in a knot, only the muscle that was in spasm was my heart.

Then the glorious heat caused the spasm to start releasing…little by little. You know that great feeling when you sense the Charlie horse letting go? You sense such relief because you know you're right around the corner from it disappearing. I felt it start loosening up, and this lovely warmth spreading across my chest, then down my arms.

I said, "It's over. I'm okay now." Jim rolled off, and I sat up and breathed deeply. Mom was glad to see the color back in my face. She asked what happened, and I replied, "My heart went into a complete quivering thing, then began to spasm and just would not beat. What horrible pain that was!"

She asked, "What in the world would cause that? You just had oral surgery today, but that went well…"

Then Mama got a funny look on her face and went to look at the pain medication bottle. She said, "Oh, my…this is what gave your grandma a heart attack years ago after surgery. You must be allergic to belladonna." (I later read that it has been known to cause the same reaction in other people as well.)

The next day, my heart felt very *sore*, like a muscle that's been pulled. I also read that is often the result of a heart attack.

I am really happy to report that I quit having frequent brushes with death and often wonder why the devil was so intent on taking me out during my early marriage. I tease my husband that his next wife wouldn't have been as patient a woman as I've been, or put up with decades of marriage with a traveling minister! Jim always answers that he married one cursed woman! (We're joking, in case that doesn't translate to the page.)

Actually I believe the enemy planned to throw my husband for a loop by making sure he'd lose his wife in early marriage to derail him from the focus his ministry has taken. I also think the devil would have preferred for our son and grandsons to have never been. (He tried to take our grandson Christian's life before he was born, and Andrew and his wife wrote about that in their booklet.)

All I know is that Jesus said, *"The thief does not come except to steal, and to kill, and to destroy. I have come that they may have life, and that they may have it more abundantly"* (John 10:10).

Whatever the reasons might be for three attacks on my life in a span of two years, I know one outcome of it all: those experiences forged an unshakable faith in the God of intervention, in the help of the Holy Spirit. If your lungs can't breathe for the sake of blood filling up inside, or your life's blood is gushing forth in a matter of minutes, or your heart just stops beating—it plain just does not phase the Lord in the least!

I'm also happy to be married to a man of faith. It has come in handy!

6

MEASURED

But to each one of us grace was given according to the measure of Christ's gift (Ephesians 4:7).

There is one Gift of God, the Lord Himself, and to each of us is given a measure of Christ's grace-gifting. That is, a grace manifesting itself as different gifts. We serve a God of variety, One who desires to express Himself in many ways.

The definition of *variety* is a "different form of a similar thing." Like different types of toothpaste at the grocery store. Colgate and Crest are both toothpastes, but with certain differences. (I like Crest myself.)

Variety is the absence of sameness or uniformity throughout; a collection of different things that share a common point. Zebras and horses are different things, but they share similarities. There are many varieties of flowers, but they are all flowers as opposed to, say, trees.

A measure of grace is given to each person in order to set the boundaries of their service within the Body. No one person has it "all" as Christ did. And that is the beauty of His design for His people, each of us with a similarity but representing the variety of Christ's gift, so that we might manifest Him in fullness collectively.

That means I need you, and you need me. This is the "sons of God." Each person being activated in their own unique gracing, working in unison to manifest the fullness of Christ's expression.

A *measure* is a particular sphere of influence, an area of activity, a territory of sorts, in which each of us is to operate. For example, a line is used to measure the distance of space between two points: from here to here is one inch. That is the area of activity for that line, one inch. Not two inches, not a foot. A graduated cylinder is used to measure the amount of a dry or liquid item between two points: from here to here is one tablespoon.

We, too, are measured. Each of us has an attribute, or certain attributes, of Christ's gift residing within us. It is through the help of the Intruder that these measures are stretched to their full potential, without crossing outside our area of influence.

> *We, however, will not boast beyond measure, but within the limits of the sphere which God appointed us—a sphere which especially includes you. For we are not overextending ourselves (as though our authority did not extend to you), for it was to you that we came with the gospel of Christ* (2 Corinthians 10:13-14).

Paul really had a dynamic understanding of this variety within the Body: *"There are differences of ministries, but the same Lord. And there are diversities of activities, but it is the same God who works all in all. But the manifestation of the Spirit is given to each one for the profit of all"* (1 Cor. 12:5-7).

And again: *"For as the body is one and has many members, but all the members of that one body, being many, are one body, so also is Christ. For by one Spirit we were all baptized into one body—whether Jews or Greeks, whether slaves or free—and have all been made to drink into one Spirit. For in fact the body is not one member but many"* (1 Cor. 12:12-14).

In fact, read that whole twelfth chapter of First Corinthians. Note the context of the variety of gifts of the Spirit is in the context of each member of the Body operating in his or her level of expression in diversity.

This measure that has been given to each of us comes from one Spirit, aggressively working within us to be activated, equipped, and sent forth to express that line of grace to the world at large, within a particular sphere of influence. Wouldn't we all agree that, say, Reinhard Bonnke's variety of gift-grace is salvation through the miraculous within the sphere of Africa? I'm just using him as a concrete example; we could pick any number of ministers and compile a similar thought, identifying the particular gifting in the particular area that sets them apart (and yet part of the same whole) from another minister. I should also point out the "sphere of influence" need not be specifically geographical (often it is)—but it could be within a particular arena of life, like "an apostolic businessperson." Their area of influence would be within the marketplace.

There are three facets to this measure of grace the Spirit is working to activate within us. The measure of gifting, the measure of rule, and the measure of faith. The combination of these three components is what determines how people respond to us as servants of God. Indeed, the Lord causes others to respond to a person's gift: *"A man's gift makes room for him, and brings him before great men"* (Prov. 18:16). In other words, a person's gift makes place for that person within God's structure of authority.

The first facet is simply what describes one's specific measure of gifting in the Word or administration: *"Let the elders who rule well be counted worthy of double honor, especially those who labor in the word and doctrine"* (1 Tim. 5:17).

The measure of rule, the second aspect, describes our specific position of authority, the area of operation. *"Each one's work will become clear; for the Day will declare it, because it will be revealed by fire; and the fire will test each one's work, of what sort it is*" (1 Cor. 3:13). We'll discuss what that "Day" is a little later.

"And God has appointed these in the church: first apostles, second prophets, third teachers, after that miracles, then gifts of healings, helps, administrations, varieties of tongues" (1 Cor. 12:28). Again, this speaks to the measure of rule. Where each person fits in.

Third, the measure of faith describes a person's attitude of confidence in moving in that gift and area of authority: *"For I say, through the grace given to me, to everyone who is among you, not to think of himself more highly than he ought to think, but to think soberly, as God has dealt to each one a measure of faith"* (Rom. 12:3).

Again, that noun word "measure" is *metron* (Strong's #3358, "mehtron") in the Greek. In Romans 12 verse 6, Paul says, *"Having then gifts differing according to the grace that is given to us, let us use them: if prophecy, let us prophesy in proportion to our faith."* The word "proportion" is *analogia* (Strong's #356, "ah-nah-law-gee-ah"), a compound word of "each [man]" and *logos* (Strong's #3056, "lah-goss"), which we should recognize as "word," representing the thoughts and mandates of God made manifest to humankind.

Of course, Jesus is the *Logos* (Word) of God—the complete, total revelation of God's thought process (His plan for humanity) summed as God Himself revealed, or clothed, in the flesh. Thus, *analogia* is the various manifestations (different parts) of the Word given to each person, a proportion of Christ's gift represented by this person, this person, this person.... This is why the eye cannot say to the hand, "I don't need you!" (see 1 Cor. 12:21). Each member of the body is vital to the complete *Logos*.

Paul is not speaking just of prophecy in Romans 12:6, and in fact, in the King James, "let us prophesy" is in parentheses, implying, "Having then gifts differing according to the grace that is given to us, let us use them...in proportion to our faith," and one of those gifts being prophecy.

The measure of *gift* is a specific gifting (that is, anointing) of God's Word with a specific effect. Whereas, the measure of *rule* is a specific authority based on a specific function (that is, responsibility). That's a lot of specifics there; please make sure you read it right.

The measure of *gift* influences the Body through the anointing of a specific gift without any reference to establishing a permanent relationship between the person with the gift and the recipient of that gift. Whereas, the measure of *rule* influences the Body through a specific position of authority that is established in the context of a permanent relationship between the people. Again, please note the differences arising from the expression of this gift of Christ measured to each one of us.

The purpose of defining these modes of operation, along with the measure of faith principle, is to show just *what* the Spirit is working toward through us. As we step into this manifestation of the sons of God, with the help of the Holy Spirit, we must grasp our abilities (measure of His gifts and anointings working through us) and "lines of demarcation" (areas of influence and opportunity).

In truth, I have sadly met many, many Christians who struggle under a frustration because they feel called to "this or that"—some specific area of activity or some specific grace calling—and yet seem stunted or thwarted in the execution of those measures. Most of the time (but not always) this frustration simply stems from a lack of understanding of their gifting, their area of rule, or the faith in fulfilling what they feel their calling may be. In other words, if you're a missionary to China, and that is not your gracing or area of authority, you're bound to run into frustrations as the enemy tries to pick you apart.

This is the work of the Holy Spirit, and our yielding to His aggressive actions in our lives, to sift through misconceptions of our measures, or trying to work outside the circles God has gifted to us. We must understand that no one particular work, anointing, or sphere of influence is less vital to the fullness of Christ's manifestation in these times. Not all of us are Pauls, not all of us are Stephens, not all of us are Peters or Philips.

The key is to find that specific anointing, our measure of gift, that specific area of operation, our measure of rule, while allowing the Spirit to activate our measure of faith in order to express that unique "thing" only we can express to the world as the collective body of Christ. This is how His fame is spread, and this is for what the glorious Intruder is pursuing us. Let us work with Him! Let us embrace His call, so that our election is sure!

> *Therefore, brethren, be even more diligent to make your call and election sure, for if you do these things you will never stumble; for so an entrance will be supplied to you abundantly into the everlasting kingdom of our Lord and Savior Jesus Christ. For this reason I will not be negligent to remind you always of these things, though you know and are established in the present truth* (2 Peter 1:10-12).

Just as Abram had to embrace the call of God to follow Him to a land He would show him, we too must embrace the call He has for us, and work with His Spirit to actualize that in our lives. We must follow the divine order of progressing into the purposes of God. We know His master plan, His purposes in Creation, are ever-unfolding.

The trumpet of God is sounding forth for His chosen to gather together and receive their marching orders, after a fashion. He is preparing us for war! He is calling, gathering, positioning, and we must embrace the call. All who will come, come!

> *David therefore departed from there and escaped to the cave of Adullam. So when his brothers and all his father's house heard it, they went down there to him. And everyone who was in distress, everyone who was in debt, and everyone who was discontented*

gathered to him. So he became captain over them. And there were about four hundred men with him (1 Samuel 22:1-2).

Those who were in distress, in debt, or discontented—they gathered unto David in preparation for battle. Do we know anyone who is in distress, in debt, or discontented? Those with infirmity (weakness) of flesh? I daresay we do.

But we must have put within us a heart toward God, ears to hear, courage to do battle, dedication, discipline, determination. These are must-haves for those who've come to gather together.

There are three P's to this concept: *a purpose, a preparation, and a provision* to see this calling succeed. We are called, assembled, as the sons of God for the mark of His approval to be upon us, just as it was on Abram. The Lord is sanctified (set apart) and we will be sanctified, too, for He cannot manifest Himself through us if we are "mixed." Embracing this call is embracing the work of the Holy Spirit to separate us, sheep from goats (His people from the world), and even sheep from sheep (as we've seen in the part about being measured in our gifts and authority).

Problem is, in many saints' lives, a foundation of "present truth" hasn't been properly laid. The purpose of the Intruder's work is to restore that foundation of truth, of ministry, of anointing.

If we want to rule and reign, well, then we need the overwhelming help of the Holy Spirit; we need the prophetic operating in our lives through that same Spirit, for it is through this operation that the "ways" are prepared, made straight. (The means, the paths we are to take; see Isaiah 40:1-3, as John the Baptist proclaimed the way of the Lord, according to Malachi 4.) See, the people are equipped, primed, and organized for this manifestation of Jesus Christ by the prophetic.

If we want to rule and reign, that divine order of progression must be restored, moving into those purposes of God by the Spirit's power. I mean, before we receive *power*, we must have a measure of *approval*. (That's a bit of the *"lest I come and smite..."* part of Malachi 4—a distinct lack of approval.) We must experience those measures of authority and power we were discussing earlier; we must press through whatever burdens or contentions (let's say, our "former experiences," either good or bad) and continue onto the path the Lord will show us. This is the second P, the preparation part. As our purposes are made known (laid straight, might be a good way to phrase it) through the activity of the Spirit's intercession in our lives, we must embrace the sanctification, the selection, the *election*, of that same Spirit.

We must be prepared, setting ourselves apart (sanctification) as the Spirit brings those leaders in who have been chosen (selection) to initiate these Body-wide moves of God (like the manifestation of the sons of God, for example). We must align ourselves with those leaders who recognize there's this move of the Spirit coming. Certain seasons of our lives should be dedicated to this process (election) of being anointed, being appointed, being set apart for the approval of God on us, so that His glory might rest upon us and shine forth through us. Indeed, that we get to a point, with the Spirit's intrusions, that we are groomed for "warfare ministry"—the aggressive acts of the Spirit that prepare the manifestation of the Lord, His fame spreading to a level we've not seen before.

This call to ingather will separate us into two camps: those who are able to wage war, and those who are not able. I believe there is a coming separation within the Church for those who don't have a heart for this type of warfare ministry. I'm not necessarily saying they leave or backslide, but they will make it clear they're not "cut out" for this type of intercession from the Spirit, and sadly, they will miss out on some of the most powerful acts of God in the past two thousand years.

We must allow God to take away everything that is a weakness so that His Spirit can strengthen us into these weapons of warfare, vessels of manifestation. This "taking away" is like pulling up weeds, those flaws and root problems that plague us. This is a must, for if you don't get rid of them, they can get rid of you!

But more than removing infirmity, we must allow God to fortify and guard our *strengths* that we do possess, for a strength unguarded will become a double-weakness. We are being established with a spirit of excellence, uncompromising, and prepared to spread that fame of Jesus far and wide.

> *When the Most High divided their inheritance to the nations, when He separated the sons of Adam, He set the boundaries of the peoples according to the number of the children of Israel* (Deuteronomy 32:8).

We are being established in boundaries of our influence, much like we discussed previously. There is a supernatural repositioning of the Body so we are standing in our proper borderlines. This territory of functionality goes back to establishing the purposes of God— we're moved where He needs us, perhaps even geographically, but I'm speaking about the realigning of our giftings, talents, our attitudes to fit our personality profiles, to maximize our efficiency in spreading the fame of Jesus. God wants His gifts drawn out of His people; otherwise, what's the purpose of giving gifts if they remain wrapped up? Supernatural alignment produces deliverance that propels you and me into God's purposes within our regions, geographically and spiritually.

I'm contacted quite frequently by dear saints who are seeking God's will for their lives. It usually pertains to some form of ministry they feel they are called to, and they ask for words of wisdom about how to proceed with this calling. Usually asking how do they operate in ministry, be that full time or alongside their daily careers?

To assist this discovery, as the Spirit works through us, intrudes in these areas of our lives that must be realigned (and we all have these areas!), we are wise to ask ourselves a number of questions throughout this process. We don't want to hamper His help!

I tell these people to ask themselves:

Is the Father pleased with what He sees in my life? Ask the Spirit to show you those things that may be not necessarily sin, but weights and hindrances, darkened areas of understanding (and we all have these areas too!). *Is the Father pleased with how He sees me minister in whatever function currently, full time or as a lay person? Is the Father pleased with the release of the giftings I have? (Holy Spirit, show me where I need improvement in unwrapping the gifts I already have.) Where can I bring the Father the most honor? Is that in itinerating, in the local church, in my job, in my home?* And perhaps most importantly, *How can I bring joy to the Father's heart in my obedience?*

These questions help identify how we are to enter into an expression of ministry. Are we team builders? Do we assist others in our lives by bringing them into *their* full potentials? That is the nature of a minister-servant heart. Or perhaps, are we entrepreneurs? Do we have ways to create new avenues, come up with new ideas that help create an environment for others to grow? It's not just a business owner's ability to tithe to the kingdom—as vitally important as that is—but it's the ability to think "outside the box." To offer services that they find are lacking in their spheres of influence.

Are we engineers? Do we have insight that helps solve problems? Can we create solutions that benefit the people around us?

Some are bridge-builders. By that I mean, we're conflict solvers, negotiators. Some of us have real giftings that serve the Body, serve the population, with the unique ability to patch up wounded relationships, broken trusts. These are the mediators.

Some are visionary in capacity. They create the concept, but not necessarily the ways and means to execute that concept. They have an idea; they need others to help plan for realizing this idea. Some others are directional; they lay out those plans step by step. Then there are the strategists, those with the distinct aptitude to develop the process for implementing the idea.

Management skills, motivational skills, shepherding, and counseling giftings: all of these are forms of serving our areas of operation, embracing the calls that God has given to each of us individually. There are different dimensions of the calling of the Lord.

The Holy Spirit works in us to unwrap these gifts; and as we allow Him to help us, He will make the means available to release those gifts. Again, otherwise what's the point of having them?

This is the selection process; opportunities that are going to be presented to us. Special timings, those appointed times we always hear about in charismatic circles, the release of our talents. God is calling forth the Elishas to pour out His Spirit upon them—the Intruder is coming. And remember: to whom God appoints—He anoints; to whom God sends—He defends.

SO HOW DO YOU KNOW?

There are principles that underscore the calling we are to embrace. First, the calling is divinely implanted by God. It is offered to favored people—those under God's grace. If we lose that sense of favor, that is, His grace—we end up prostituting our ministries. And how sad is that?

Ministry once revealed cannot be hidden—it has to manifest. Ministry needs to mature continually. If it doesn't, it becomes stunted, retarded; and it is *possible* that God may have to remove it. Note I said it's possible, not "without question." But look, when ministry begins, it's maintained by an intimate relationship with the Lord. This retardation does *not* have to happen.

For some examples on the call to ministry, read about Samuel as a child in First Samuel 3; Elisha's call as a man while plowing, (see 1 Kings 19:19-21); Jeremiah's call, even before he was conceived! (see Jer. 1:5); Amos' call to prophesy while he was a herdsman and a grower of figs (see Amos 1:1; 7:12-14).

So how do you know you're called? Good question. There are certain principles for all levels of callings. First, there can be supernatural events, visitations from angels or the Lord Himself: *"In the year that King Uzziah died, I saw the Lord sitting on a throne, high and lifted up, and the train of His robe filled the temple"* (Isa. 6:1; see also Jer. 1:4, and again 1 Sam. 3:1-4).

Other ways? People will begin to tell you you're called—once more see First Samuel 3, specifically verse 20. The leadership in the church will recognize it (see Prov. 18:16). Others may receive an initial prophecy about their future callings, like Jeremiah, Samuel, Zechariah (see Acts 13:1-3, 2 Tim. 1:6). God will confirm His word (see 2 Cor. 13:1). Fruit will begin to bear (see Mark 16:20).

So the last will be first, and the first last. For many are called, but few chosen (Matthew 20:16).

That word "chosen" (and the same in Matt. 22:14) is more often translated "elect" in the New Testament. But the Greek word for both is *eklektos* (Strong's #1588, "eck-leck-toss") and comes from a root meaning "to call out" appropriately enough. It means "picked out, chosen" and applies to all Christians individually as those who are secure in salvation.

But it also can apply to the choicest, the select (the best of the class, so to speak). Preeminent excellence "applied to certain individual Christians." Not everyone is "chosen" in this sense, even though they are all born-again Christians.

I make this distinction because I want to point out here, when discussing "calling and election," that I am not just specifically speaking of one's salvation experience. I believe that is secure the moment we confess with our mouths and believe in our hearts (see Rom. 10:9), and it is open to every person on this planet drawing breath. I do not believe God creates souls for the specific purpose of going to hell.

But when discussing "calling and election," I am not trying to argue with Reformed theologists, nor those who hold a once-saved-always-saved stance, nor those who adhere to an ultra-Calvinistic predestination concept.

I am talking about being one of the elect as a "highly favored" Christian, the "select" or top-of-the-class—assuming the salvation experience is already a done deal, whether they were chosen, or chose themselves.

Once a person has come to Christ, or was chosen to come to Christ, or whatever viewpoint there may be out there—no matter *how* they came to Christ, once they have—I believe He has something He wants them to do. So remember "calling and election" are dealing with destinies *after* salvation, not the act of getting saved itself, for that is already settled—at least, in the context of this discussion here.

In this context then, we know His calling before being chosen (this is the election principle discussed earlier). What does this mean, really? We know we have a purpose He wants fulfilled; how do we make ourselves available to become one of the elect, "highly favored" bunch? How do we become "chosen"?

Look, God is fashioning us into warring instruments—this is the aggressive nature of the Spirit we are talking about here. He wants to use us as a "surgical strike" on the cutting edge of humanity's needs to manifest the truth of His Son's gospel.

The security of our election (God's choosing us—after we have been born again) stems from faith in His promises and growing in the fruit of His Spirit. We allow the Intruder to work within us to make our election sure.

You have a calling, something God wants you to do, something you need to accomplish. You're not here just to look good and float through life until you meet Jesus in heaven. Working with the Spirit's intercession places you in a position to fulfill that calling.

Hey, we know salvation of the eternal soul is by faith and grace, not works; but faith without works is dead (see James 2:17). God expects something from us after we've been ransomed from the kingdom of darkness. You have a calling. He wants you to fulfill that calling, whatever it may be. It is up to you to work with the Spirit to make that calling, and thereby your election, secure (again, not *salvation*, I mean, election as being one of the highly favored sons of God).

So what does that mean, that many are called, few are chosen? What does it mean when Peter talks about our "call and election" being sure? (See Second Peter 1, from the start of this chapter.) By adding all those things to our faith (virtue, knowledge, self-control, perseverance, godliness, brotherly kindness and love—note the similarity to the fruit of the Spirit in Galatians 5), Peter assures us that *"if you do these things you will never stumble"* (2 Pet.1:10).

These things are what keep us "saved" (in the sense of a vibrant, living relationship with God's Spirit, the fulfillment of His calling on your life—I'm not saying "dying and going to hell," although I think we would be unwise to preclude this in the most extreme cases, but again I'm not picking a fight with the once-saved-always-saved group).

We should understand the difference between *calling* and *election*. Calling is our actions that prove our election (being chosen, favored), which is our motives behind the actions. Yes, that's cyclical, because one goes hand in hand with the other. You are saved (election, chosen); now you will act out God's purposes in your life (calling). Otherwise the faith is dead; that is, not producing fruit, not breathing, not vibrant. You are not saved *only* to be saved.

The election part is not what saves you, we're talking about something after the getting saved part—we need to see beyond just the concept of salvation for our immortal souls (which is, of course, the most important part; but subsequently, it is also to *lead* you into your calling beyond your salvation experience). It's not just that the few who are "chosen" are the ones who go to heaven, and the other ones don't—we're talking about fulfilling the purposes God has for our lives after we come to Him. Many who are saved do not fulfill the calling God has placed on their lives. And this is sad.

In other words, Peter subjoins election to calling because the calling is the effect and proof of God's election (choosing us). Calling is the *expression* of our purpose, and *purpose* is our election, His choosing us for one of the highly favored. Many are indeed called, but few get to the point of fulfilling God's purposes that they are chosen.

This is not God's fault. He is no respecter of persons (see Rom. 2:11). He does not pick and choose who will be "highly favored." He's not up there playing favorites with the saints. What is available to one of His children is equally available to all of His children. But it is *our* response to the work of the Holy Spirit within us that places us in a position to take advantage of being one of the "chosen" of God.

Calling is the fruit in action, the faith with works. We know the Spirit's calling before we know His election. As we work out the calling, we encounter the election. And if we neglect either one, we may stumble. How we stay "saved" (again, I don't mean just "not going to hell") or healed or delivered or secured, how we remain steadfast, is directly related to allowing the Spirit to guide us through our calling and into our election.

Paul, in Romans 12, outlines several principles, those things to which the Spirit is calling us, training us, commissioning us to fulfill: prophecy, ministry, teaching, exhorting, giving, ruling, showing mercy, loving, filled with brotherly love, preferring others above ourselves, serving, not being slothful, rejoicing, patience in adversity, continuing in prayer, charity, hospitality, etc. Note verse 11, *"fervent in spirit."* I like that one.

We are all born with a certain gift, even before we are saved. This is a motivational gift, what drives us—even those in the world have this kind of gift. "I knew from a young age I wanted to be a doctor." It is a product of being born.

And then we are born again with a gift, let's say, occasionally, but then we are baptized in the Spirit with a gift *especially* so. Again, there is a progression in God here. We all have callings, and the fulfillment of those callings are gradual, emerging throughout the course of our lives (and new lives in Christ), some even becoming apparent later in life. So if you're fifteen or fifty-five, you have a calling. We are sovereignly called before we are even born. God then leaves it up to us to work with His Spirit to ensure our election.

Let's take the prophetic as a specific example. You may ask yourself, *How do I know I'm called to the prophetic?* Well, your motivational gift—what drives you—will be to want to prophesy. It's an in-born desire. As you progress in your relationship with the Spirit, the word of knowledge, the word of wisdom, simple prophecy will begin to function in your life.

Ah, but let's progress further—perhaps it's deeper, this calling to be prophetic, and you may ask yourself, *How do I know I'm called **as a prophet*** in the Ephesians 4:11 sense of standing in the office of a prophet, equipping the saints in the prophetic. Well, you'll feel called to full-time ministry as a profession, not just utilizing a gift of prophecy in a church setting on occasion. You'll feel a desire for pulpit ministry, preaching the gospel. And you will progress in your ministry release through the course of your life as you work with the Spirit's movings. Just as an associate pastor moves into the role of a senior pastor. You start street evangelizing and progress into international crusades. And so on.

This may be oversimplifying the concept, but I want to show that this progression is marked, initiated, and completed through the help of the Holy Spirit. We *must* embrace the calling of God on our lives, work with the Intruder, and make our elections sure.

I'd like to say that God is taking those who have sinned against the prophetic operation to the waters of separation. Just like Gideon's army (see Judg. 7). Those who "lap the water" are chosen, you know what I mean? The *thirsty!* Those who get after the water like dogs, not prim and proper, kneeling just so.

Those who have purposely or ignorantly neglected His Spirit moving in their lives, downplayed His gifts, including tongues—those who've hampered the aggressive moves of the Spirit—those who've bucked against the glorious Intruder. Those who will not "add to their faith…." These, and their heart issues, their attitudes, and motives, will be separated from the lapping warriors.

> *And Joshua said to the people, "Sanctify yourselves, for tomorrow the Lord will do wonders among you"* (Joshua 3:5).

For those of us lapping at the water's edge, the Intruder is saying our time in the wilderness draws short. Like Romans 12 points out, we have different gifts (calling) according to the grace (election) given us—so by all means, let's use them! We've been in the ministry, waiting on our ministering (Rom. 12:7 KJV). For the Spirit has moved upon us to reveal and show us what's really in our hearts.

Now, add to this faith, virtue, to this virtue, knowledge…add all these to your calling, and you will not stumble in your election. As we grow in our understanding of these measures, gifts, spheres of influence by the help of the Spirit, and as we press into operating in them, it will develop a greater yielding of confidence for the Lord to entrust to us His greater fullness of sonship ministry and anointing.

Thus is His fame spread throughout the earth!

7

DEMONSTRATION

IF YOU'VE READ THE PROPHETS IN THE OLD TESTAMENT, AND even the references in the New Testament, you know about this Day of the Lord. It's a pretty common phrase, even way back in Amos' time (see Amos 5:18-20), and it usually means a time of the Lord's wrath poured out to chasten His wayward people or those who reject Him. It is when the Lord has become fed up with the way humanity is acting. This "Day" (see 2 Pet. 3:8-10) is a period of judgment, and throughout history there have been several "Days"— but there is also a future Day of the Lord. He will be vindicated, ultimately on *the* Day (that is, the Second Coming of Christ), so there are eschatological revelations concerning the Day of the Lord as well.

It is coming. And even though gross darkness will cover the face of the earth (again, see Isa. 60:2), in that Day the glorious Intruder will be poured out on all flesh. (Keep in mind I'm talking about several fulfillments of the "Day of the Lord"—He has *already* been poured out, and He will be poured out afresh.)

And it shall come to pass afterward that I will pour out My Spirit on all flesh; your sons and your daughters shall prophesy, your old men shall dream dreams, your young men shall see visions. And also on My menservants and on My maidservants I will pour out My Spirit in those days. And I will show wonders in the heavens and in the earth: blood and fire and pillars of smoke. The sun shall be turned into darkness, and the moon into blood, before the coming of **the great and awesome day of the Lord**. *And it shall come to pass that* **whoever calls on the name of the Lord shall be saved**. *For in Mount Zion and in Jerusalem there shall be deliverance, as the Lord has said, among the remnant whom the Lord calls* (Joel 2:28-32).

Most of us miss the context of the Intruder being poured out: in the midst of earthly turmoil and tribulation. So here's the sun dark, the moon blood; I mean, all this blood and fire and smoke—yet in the midst of this outpouring of wrath, these wonders in the heavens and in the earth, there is also the outpouring of the Spirit, and whoever (that means anyone) calls upon the name of the Lord will be saved.

This is a coming Day of Demonstration. And you and I are to have a part in it. This is the ministry of the New Testament, the ministry of the glorious—indeed the ministry of the Spirit by the manifestation of truth.

Therefore, since we have this ministry, as we have received mercy, we do not lose heart. But we have renounced the hidden things of shame, not walking in craftiness nor handling the word of God deceitfully, but by manifestation of the truth commending ourselves to every man's conscience in the sight of God. But even if our gospel is veiled, it is veiled to those who are perishing, whose minds the god of this age has blinded, who do not believe, lest the **light of the gospel of the glory of Christ**, *who is the image of God, should shine on them. ...And since we have the same spirit of faith, according to what is written, "I believed and therefore I spoke," we also believe and therefore speak...* (2 Corinthians 4:1-4,13).

The release of the anointing is truth manifested. You'll recall Second Peter 1:12 speaks about this "present truth," that is, truth at hand, truth for the time we are in: a new aspect of well-established scriptural truth that comes to the forefront, receiving a Spirit-inspired focus at a specific moment in time. Truth in the present. It encloses us, surrounds us, encompasses us, this truth; and we are to demonstrate the Spirit of truth poured out on all flesh.

This is the context of Joel 2, the dreams, the prophecies, the visions, the signs and wonders that are the *"light of the gospel of the glory of Christ."* The manifestation of truth is the manifestation of reality, and it comes in the midst of the dark Day of the Lord.

> *Therefore let that* [truth] *abide in you which you heard from the beginning. If what you heard from the beginning abides in you, you also will abide in the Son and in the Father* (1 John 2:24—but read the context before verse 24; John is speaking of truth).

It is the truth that produces genuine astonishment (there is false astonishment, too, we'll see this in just a moment). Genuine astonishment is created when authority is executed to release the supernatural through the help of the Holy Spirit, and this is how the fame of Christ is spread: the manifestation of *Truth* (see Mark 1:21-28, specifically verse 22).

This is what Jesus is talking about when He says, *"And you shall know the truth, and the truth shall make you free"* (John 8:32). But it is the truth that you *know* that makes you free. It is truth exhibited, expressed, a bestowment, a gift. Not a concept of truth, but truth in reality, known truth, present truth.

So, if Jesus shared a truth about joy (see John 15:11)—there was an expression of *joy* that the people listening experienced. The truth of joy was *manifested*. And this is what created the astonishment, spreading His fame. When Jesus taught "peace" (see John 14:27; 16:33) as the Prince of Peace (see Isa.9:6)—those listening *experienced* the truth of peace. They entered into a heightened state of awareness to understand just what the Lord was saying about peace.

The Holy Spirit is poured out upon us to move aggressively in our midst so that we might experience the manifestation of truth in any particular attribute of God; be that salvation, healing, deliverance, a word of knowledge, panoramic operation, and so on.

But if there is a lack of the manifestation of truth, it creates a veiling of deception. God is slandered and misrepresented, the people are not made free, for they do not *know* the truth. We need to give them a revelation (see Eph. 1:17-21), an unveiling, of the manifested presence of God—hence His "wonders in the heavens and in the earth." Hey, there really is God up here, stop messing around!

Quite so, for *"the manifestation of the Spirit is given to each one for the profit of all"* (1 Cor. 12:7) and *"when He, the Spirit of truth, has come, He will guide you into all truth; for He will not speak on His own authority, but whatever He hears He will speak; and He will tell you things to come"* (John 16:13).

Jesus was saying, "The Spirit of truth will hear of My activity and will show you these things to come." The Spirit will *guide* us into all truth. That speaks of His work *behind* the truth, making it real and tangible to us. This is the help of the Holy Spirit.

We need a genuine display of the divine, for no manifestation of the truth creates a vacuum. Without the authentic display, the door is opened to the counterfeit, the imitation of the divine. This is rampant in today's society, and this is barreling us toward the "Day" of the Lord. We must align ourselves with the Spirit of truth to present the reality of God, not in a theoretic way—but with *astonishment* at the authority of the doctrine, a tangible display that brings an unveiling of God's truth.

"When all that generation had been gathered to their fathers, another generation arose after them who did not know the Lord nor the work

which He had done for Israel" (Judg. 2:10). Sound familiar? Gideon knew the *truth* was missing.

> *Gideon said to Him, "O my lord, if the Lord is with us, why then has all this happened to us? And where are all His miracles which our fathers told us about, saying, 'Did not the Lord bring us up from Egypt?' But now the Lord has forsaken us and delivered us into the hands of the Midianites"* (Judges 6:13)

> *But I fear, lest somehow, as the serpent deceived Eve by his craftiness, so your minds may be corrupted from the simplicity that is in Christ. For if he who comes preaches another Jesus whom we have not preached, or if you receive a different spirit which you have not received, or a different gospel which you have not accepted—you may well put up with it!* (2 Corinthians 11:3-4).

Another generation. Another spirit. And have we put up with it? I say, long enough. People need the supernatural. But as much, people need it in line with the Word (see Matt. 22:29). The supernatural without the Word opens the door to deception, sensationalism. This is not good. Yet, the Word without the supernatural *can* (not *must)* leave us doubting (see 2 Cor. 3:6).

In the Day of the Lord, people *will* be confronted with the supernatural. But if we are not demonstrating a manifestation of the truth in line with the Word, they *can* (not *must)* become sidetracked with false representation of the divine, an imitation. Sound familiar? Just as the Spirit will initiate a divine invasion, intruding upon the world with *truth*, there will be a counter-invasion from the pagan/ New Age/mystical camp.

TWOS

So you and I only have two options. Will we become truth-manifesting sons of God? Will our lives become a miracle? Or will our lives become a maze of confusion and deception? Take the first choice. Cast off the major obsessions of humankind today, the materialism, the garbage and filth that deludes and deceives and veils the truth of God.

For I proclaim in the near future, in this Day of the Lord, there will be only *two* major obsessions the world will have: the pursuit of God or the wave of the occult. These lying signs and wonders will cause many to embrace counterfeits and substitutes—quite literally they will be baptized into black magic. Not just "black magic"—but false religions and cults, not just blatantly occult.

Don't be deceived, children of God!

There are *two* forms of the supernatural: God's truth manifested in signs, wonders and miracles, and that maze of confusion and deception (technically, I define this as "preternatural").

There are *two* ways people arrive at a "spiritual" conclusion. Conviction: they are convicted by the manifestation of the truth. Or seduction: they are seduced by a lie. They are brought under the element of either one or the other. It's not just the "signs and wonders"—it is the heart issues behind the signs and wonders. Pharaoh's wizards had magic; Aaron's was the rod of truth (see Exod. 7:7-13). Both were "supernatural," but in the end, the manifested truth swallowed the lie.

Look, people are tormented. They're being driven to find new, exotic answers for the reasons why they are tormented. The false supernatural gives them "answers" as it lies to them. It is a bad nature that says, "I want to arrive at a spiritual experience any way I can." Without the Word and the Spirit, the truth in demonstration, they are tricked into believing what they see through the modern spiritists, mediums, and psychics, what have you, is "the real deal." And the torment continues.

But know this, that in the last days perilous times will come…
evil men and impostors will grow worse and worse, deceiving
and being deceived (2 Timothy 3:1,13).

Now the Spirit expressly says that in latter times some will depart
from the faith, giving heed to deceiving spirits and doctrines of
demons (1 Timothy 4:1).

Let me expound upon this notion that "some will depart." The concept here is not just one huge "bam!" experience and you've departed from the faith. It's little by little, by degrees. The idea is someone taking you by the hand and gently leading you off track. The Greek literally means "to be led off the path." If people knew they were being deceived, they wouldn't be deceived.

The King James for those two Timothy passages uses the words seducers and seducing. The Greek is synonymous for sorcerers, enchanters: literally meaning a wailer, a howler (because magical incantations were uttered in a howling voice), a juggler, a nomad, rover, vagabond, a wanderer (leading another off the path, see). To corrupt, to deceive. An imposter. Quite specifically it means "a tramp"—a hobo who takes another off the main path and out into the wilds. To be bewitched, enchanted, seduced. A soothsayer. A clairvoyant, mystic, fortune-teller, oracle, astrologer, star-reader. These are seducers.

I call this "high risk living." In the last of the last days, these coming years will be difficult, to say the least. Each new decade as we rush toward the Day of the Lord will add a measure of danger, risk, and new hurts.

Paul continues to admonish Timothy just what these evil people are all about:

For men will be lovers of themselves, lovers of money, boasters,
proud, blasphemers, disobedient to parents, unthankful, unholy,
unloving, unforgiving, slanderers, without self-control, brutal,

despisers of good, traitors, headstrong, haughty, lovers of pleasure rather than lovers of God, having a form of godliness but denying its power. And from such people turn away! For of this sort are those who creep into households and make captives of gullible women loaded down with sins, led away by various lusts, always learning and never able to come to the knowledge of the truth (2 Timothy 3:2-7).

This is "casting off natural affection," and being so self-centered and selfish as to indulge in all of those things the apostle lists, a ton of horrific adjectives. And yet, "having a form of godliness," these people deny God's power, trying to stop its operation. They have an element of power; outwardly it looks real; on the surface you can't tell the difference. But the substance is not the same—deception is in their message. From such people, turn away!

These soulish-driven manifestations are used to intimidate, manipulate, and dominate a hurting people seeking answers by tapping into a pseudo-spiritual realm of "cosmic creativity," which is really the realm of fallen imaginations, expressions of the mind through the five senses, so that the hurting people will resist the truth. This is a power, but it is a false power. There is a limitation in the preternatural realm.

Now as Jannes and Jambres resisted Moses, so do these also resist the truth: men of corrupt minds, disapproved concerning the faith; but they will progress no further, for their folly will be manifest to all, as theirs also was (2 Timothy 3:8-9).

Paul is likening those people he mentions in verses 2-7 to Pharaoh's magicians in Exodus 7. (Talmudists and Rabbins have the Egyptian sorcerers traditionally named Jannes, "he vexed," and Jambres, "foamy healer;" that's where Paul got their names. Further, Jewish myth has them leaving with Moses and the Israelites, converted to Judaism, but perishing before they reached Canaan—don't know if that's true or not, but probably. I mean, if your snake-staffs had been swallowed, wouldn't *you* convert?)

That phrase "so do these also" means in the same, identical way, using the very same methods; with perfect duplication do these types "resist the truth." We're talking about a spirit of false magic. This spirit is defeated when there is a genuine display of the divine, and thus "their folly" is made manifest. Indeed, their serpents are swallowed up. The miracles themselves—true miracles—pull down the demonic manifestations.

(As an aside, I wonder why Exodus 7:12 doesn't say Aaron's serpent swallowed their serpents? It says his rod swallowed theirs. Like, what? As if the swallowing occurred *after* the serpents turned back into rods? Then that would mean the rod itself opened up to consume the other rods? Interesting.)

The point here is the "proceed no further" means stopped dead in their tracks. Completely, instantly halted. The true supernatural breaks the false preternatural. It's a shock to the seducers, for they are made to see "their folly."

Our job as truth-manifesting sons of God is to use the true miraculous to manifest the very character of God; His personage is emphasized and shatters the false supernatural.

But the point I wish to bring out in this Day of Demonstration is that an *astonishment* is not enough. Simon the Sorcerer was able to bewitch the people (see Acts 8:9-24). (Remember the Greek, *existemi*, from earlier—it's the same word here.)

It is not your *fear* of being bewitched and deceived that will keep you from being bewitched or deceived—it is only your *intimacy* with Jesus! Wherein the Lord dwells within you, cohabitates with you, you become the house of the Lord. Which segues into our next topic, but you'll have to follow me here for a bit to make the connection, okay?

Therefore, holy brethren, partakers of the heavenly calling, con-sider the Apostle and High Priest of our confession, Christ Jesus, who was faithful to Him who appointed Him, as Moses also was faithful in all His house. For this One has been counted worthy of more glory than Moses, inasmuch as He who built the house has more honor than the house. For every house is built by someone, but He who built all things is God. And Moses indeed was faith-ful in all His house as a servant, for a testimony of those things which would be spoken afterward, but Christ as a Son over His own house, **whose house we are** *if we hold fast the confidence and the rejoicing of the hope firm to the end* (Hebrews 3:1-6).

We as demonstrators in this Day are partakers of a heavenly call-ing, which is Christ Jesus—manifesting *Him* through the help of the Holy Spirit. We live for the unseen to become seen (see 2 Cor. 4:18). You might could say we're zealots, full of ardent desire to represent the truth of Jesus Christ to the world at large. That the zeal of the Lord for a true demonstration of Himself has eaten us up! Now hang in there, this will come together in a bit.

Now the Passover of the Jews was at hand, and Jesus went up to Jerusalem. And He found in the temple those who sold oxen and sheep and doves, and the money changers doing business (John 2:13-14).

Jesus goes to the temple, He sees people selling oxen and sheep, and He gets upset at them, to put it mildly. People selling a "form of godliness" for profit (the type of people Paul warned Timothy about, see?). In His zeal, He drives them out of the temple, saying, *"Do not make My Father's house a house of merchandise!"* (John 2:16). And note verse 17, *"Then His disciples remembered that it was written, 'Zeal for Your house has eaten Me up.'"* This comes from Psalm 69:9.

It shows that Jesus was jealous for His Father's honor (His glory) to be protected, and would not let it be sullied by a group of peo-ple who were basically thieves. He cherished the presence of His

Father above all else, and was vehement in protecting the house of the Lord. Just as Moses was faithful and zealous in protecting the Lord's glory and honor (see Exod. 32-33), the Lord's about to consume the people, "Stand aside, Moses, I'll make out of you a great nation…." In other words, He's really upset (to put it mildly) at the stiff-necked people, you know? But here's Moses, standing in the gap for the Israelites, beseeching the Lord to spare them, "Remember Your reputation, God—if You burn them all up, what will the Egyptians say? He did all that just to wipe them out in the desert?" Boy, Moses was a good servant.

THE GREAT THERAPIST

Let's talk about house stewards here for a second. In the Hebrews 3 passage, there is a word here used only one time in the New Testament, and it's translated "servant," speaking of Moses as a servant in the Lord's house. The Greek word is *therapon* (Strong's #2324, "the-rah-pone") and might be better translated "attendant." It stems from "to heat" as in making something warm (in this case the house—or housewarming) and incidentally is where the Greek word for "summer" came from, 'cause it's warm in summertime, see? (Thermos or thermometer are English examples—the "ther" part.)

Now *therapon* serves as the root for another Greek word, a verb that is *therapeuo* (Strong's #2323, "the-rah-poo-oh") and is translated as "heal" or "cure," and in one case "worship" (see Acts 17:25). You will recognize the English word "therapy." It implies an act of serving (as in Moses in Hebrews 3, stewarding a house, making it "warm"), ministering to someone until the person recovers wellness, stooping over someone's sickbed and nursing them back to health.

This therapy word is used to describe the healing acts of Jesus Christ. He was the great Therapist. It encompasses not only the restoration of the body, but of the mind and emotions and spirit as well. Total healing, made whole, complete healing of all things wrong with a person. So when Jesus healed the man of leprosy in Mark's Gospel, He not only cured the leprosy but all of the emotional and mental woundings that would go hand in hand with living in such a diseased state. (see Mark 1:40-45).

The connection here, then, is that the house of the Lord is to be a house of therapy. And we are to be so zealous for this kind of expression that it consumes us! This is how we overcome the deception of the sorcerers—with a manifestation of the truth that brings therapy to those who are tortured by preternatural activity.

> *As His divine power has given to us all things that pertain to life and godliness, through the knowledge of Him who called us by glory and virtue, by which have been given to us exceedingly great and precious promises, that through these you may be partakers of the divine nature, having escaped the corruption that is in the world through lust* (2 Peter 1:3-4).

Life. Virtue. Godliness and glory. Again, the word "partakers." Jesus is our heavenly calling, and being *in Him*, His divine power energizes our own lives, making us partakers of that divine nature. His High Priest and Apostolic ministry releases us into partaking (that is, "taking part") of everything that pertains to life—we are taking part in a heavenly calling!

It's as if we come into the Most High One—He lifts us up into the heavenly priesthood. This is what it means to be "in Christ." You know what that tells me? That we will not be robbed of any of the virtues and graces of Christ in our lives. So much so, that we will be the expression of that divine power in Christ on earth. For our High Priest is faithful in making us partakers of everything pertaining to His life; He is the Apostle of our profession. (Again, back to Hebrews 3:1.) He will cleave to us (see Gen. 2:24), His Bride, and He'll never stop chasing us, for we are joined together. Joint-heirs of this divine nature (see 1 Cor. 6:17). What honor! *That means you and I can minister for Jesus in the Person of Jesus from His ascension position in heaven.*

It is in the context of dynamic power (the Greek word is *dynamis*, Strong's #1411) that Peter is saying we are partakers of life and godliness: a divine nature instilled within us through the living Spirit of Christ, the glorious Intruder; thereby we experience and express these *"exceedingly great and precious promises."* Jesus is, indeed, in ministry today! He is continually revealing the nature of God (all things pertaining to life and godliness).

Psalm 37:4 says, *"Delight yourself also in the Lord, and He shall give you the desires of your heart."* What a great word—delight. It means we are to lay down our lives to Him and thoroughly adapt ourselves to the Person we are delighting in—to cleave to Him, our Husband, as His wife (the Bride). How therapeutic, to be given the desires of our hearts! Whom you delight in rubs off on you! You will never stop chasing Him, and He will never stop chasing you! The definition of *passion* is what you delight in, what you are willing to lay down everything else for, what you are willing to suffer for because it is better than everything else.

Back to Hebrews 3, that instruction to *"consider the Apostle and High Priest"* means to bring into focus our highest level of thinking. Bring all your attention to the Apostle and High Priest. Consider then our Apostle and High Priest who lives forever to make intercession on our behalves (see Heb. 7:23-25).

> *God, who at various times and in various ways spoke in time past to the fathers by the prophets, has in these last days spoken to us by His Son, whom He has appointed heir of all things, through whom also He made the worlds; who being the brightness of His glory and the express image of His person, and upholding all things by the word of His power, when He had by Himself purged our sins, sat down at the right hand of the Majesty on high, having become so much better than the angels, as He has by*

inheritance obtained a more excellent name than they (Hebrews 1:1-4).

The cross is central to everything we can lay hold to in our salvation experience through life. It is by His crucifixion we are able to have so great an Apostle, and it is His resurrection that opens the door to life and godliness. But we must also *consider* His glorification, His ascended position at the right hand of the Father. *It is His present ministry today that empowers our present ministry today, through the work of the Holy Spirit, so that we can spread His fame throughout the lands.*

Our Apostle and High Priest represents us to the Father, yes? He is the Apostle and High Priest of our *profession* or confession. Therefore, the ammunition, so to speak, that we give Jesus to represent us is what we give Him with our lips. What we speak, what we profess. What we cry out, He backs up to the Father, and says, "Do this on their behalves based on their position *in* Me through My blood." And the Father watches over those words to perform them (see Jer. 1:12). Our words *in* Christ arrest the ear of the Father through the Son's blood, and He watches to make sure they are carried out.

You know that the precious and costly blood of Jesus, as our High Priest, cries out mercy, and that the Father grants us access to His very throne room on behalf of that blood (see Heb. 4:16). Through that blood, as we confess and profess, He is faithful and just to forgive us our sins and cleanse us from all unrighteousness (see 1 John 1:9). This is *redemption*, and it is the single greatest tenet of the Christian faith. No other religion in the world comes close to touching this inestimable provision bought by the blood of the Lamb, that deity sacrificed Himself for the sake of humanity.

But that same blood of Jesus, as our Apostle, cries out in *proclamation*. Call upon Me, I will answer! It proclaims all those things of life and godliness, it declares *all* that He is, the whole conversation of the Father. The context of the passage in Hebrews 1 is that the

Father speaks *by His Son*, right? The full conversation of God the Father is in Jesus Christ; that is, the sum total of what He wants to say to humanity is said through our Lord Jesus.

As we move in the therapy of the Lord, the manifestation of the truth, we warm His house (that's us ourselves—we're good stewards of His habitation) and we entice those around us to experience this household for themselves. Thus is His fame spread.

In Christ, we are to be like trees planted by streams of waters (see Ps. 1:3; Jer. 17:8), and our leaves are to be medicine that heals the nations (see Ezek. 47:12; Rev. 22:2). We are to be therapists to them, bringing wholeness, not just physical healing, but a shocking revelation of present truth that brings them out of the stupor of false power. They will smell the aroma of life upon us. Mmmm. That smells good!

In Christ, we are sent forth to the tormented, acting, perceiving, doing, just as if He were acting, perceiving, doing Himself. The manifestation of the sons of God; these are the "greater works" He spoke of (see John 14:12). Greater in the sense of magnitude, for as He is now in an ascended, glorified position, millions across the world, at any given moment in time, may call upon Him and expect to see the same results He produced as a Man here on earth. He is manifested through His sons.

And note the very next portion of John 14 is the promise of the Helper who abides (makes His home, His abode) with us forever— the Spirit prepares us for these greater works. It gets to a point that we cannot help *but* to change people's lives, just because we've showed up. We're there, and Christ is manifested. The life of God within us expressed fully and tangibly to spread His fame to the farthest reaches of influence we have in this world.

We become a house of refuge, a sanctuary, a safe haven to the people on the outside. They are drawn and enter a state of astonishment at the present truth revealed.

This house goes everywhere we go, for it *is* us—Christ in us, His house, the complete thought of the Father's expression to the world. This house is a work of the Holy Spirit in our lives. As we yield to the Intruder, He will aggressively groom us, for lack of a better term, to be the demonstrators of truth in the midst of the Day of the Lord.

8

FACTORS

For through Him we both have access by one Spirit to the Father. Now, therefore, you are no longer strangers and foreigners, but fellow citizens with the saints and members of the household of God, having been built on the foundation of the apostles and prophets, Jesus Christ Himself being the chief cornerstone, in whom the whole building, being fitted together, grows into a holy temple in the Lord, in whom you also are being built together for a dwelling place of God in the Spirit (Ephesians 2:18-22).

Seems we see this scripture a lot; I think I've quoted some portion of it in just about every book I've written. But it is one of the best. (Well, how can you choose *the* best?) This passage is crammed with information, and specifically, it ties well into the house of therapy notes from the previous chapter, for it just proves once more we are the household of God. Living in unison with the Father, and His firstborn Son as the underpinning for the entire organization.

For what purpose? To be a dwelling place for God *in the Spirit*. The glorious Intruder inhabits and resides within this tabernacle—that's us. This building of the house is a continuing work. The point of this book is to show the Spirit's role in that building, working in perfect harmony with the Father and the Son, to complete a perfect household around the globe. The ultimate function of this building project is to expand its borders to everyone who will choose to come live in the house. So we work to spread the fame of the chief Cornerstone to any and all who will listen and see.

Not just listen, but *see* the manifestation of the Son in truth and power. I am a power evangelist. I do not believe that all people throughout the world, many of them misled by a false notion of God as an angry taskmaster, or an uncaring floating presence out there in the cosmos, are to adhere to the gospel without *any* kind of representation that *this* gospel is the real way to God. So a release of the supernatural aspect of the Spirit in a tangible way provides a confrontation to those who are lost: *"choose for yourselves this day whom you will serve"* (Josh. 24:15).

So the whole of this book up till now has been to help show you that the Helper is grooming you as a member of the household to go out in the highways and the byways (see Luke 14:23) to present the truth in manifestation to others. In other words, this is a book on evangelism, as much as it is a book on any other topic.

SOULS

The whole point, the whole thrust, the whole passion of our day-to-day operation should be gathering souls. Now I'll be branded a soul-solicitor by the average atheistic, humanistic person on the street. That's true. Absolutely guilty. I believe in God, I believe there is a hell, and whatever I have to do, whatever the Spirit has to reveal in manifestation to prove that—then that's what I want to see happen.

It always seems to come down to money, doesn't it? You share your beliefs with a co-worker, and immediately they think you're trying to recruit them into a Kool-Aid drinking cult to pilfer their pockets for your local church's coffers. No way you could actually be altruistic, just trying once again to convince them that if their heart stopped in the middle of the night, they'd instantly be in eternal torment. So they think you're crazy or money-mongering.

I'll minister to hundreds of people until one in the morning, just exhausted, ready to collapse into bed, and guaranteed there's a tiny percentage of the audience that thinks I'm doing all this for an extra $100. Well, fine. You're going to believe what you want. And yes, a man's gotta feed his family. But there are much easier ways to make money than being a full-time itinerant minister—and much more lucrative ways, too! I could've been a football player. Or a fighter pilot. Man, sometimes I wish I were a car salesman…

No. I'm only kidding. I do all this because I am desperately persuaded that if the Christians in the congregation are hurting, needing therapy themselves, they are hampered in their God-given quest to expand the household out there in the world. They need to be equipped to reproduce the works of the Spirit in the streets, thereby spreading the fame of the Lord.

And I pray just one person, one lost soul, will see me minister past midnight and *believe* I'm sincere, choosing to accept my words as right and true—and save him or herself from hellfire (see John 10:38, 14:11). There's nothing wrong with getting saved because you don't want to go to hell! After that, the Spirit will work on you to create the love for salvation, faith toward God. But He'll start with fear of damnation, too. Whatever it takes.

The reason why God the Spirit works through us to spread the witness of Jesus Christ is to bring about an admiration of the Father God. The Lord desires to be worshiped by humanity—otherwise, what is the point of being God? And of course, it is in our best interest to worship Him. Again, it's all about winning souls.

Okay, so if this book up till now has been about evangelism, what are some of the underlying foundations, key *factors* that the Spirit uses to equip us as soul-solicitors? What are some of the ways we become these witnesses of Jesus' manifestation?

Witness. That's a good word. In the Greek forms, all the words for witness, testimony, record come from the root *martys* (Strong's #3144, "mar-tuse") where we get the English word martyr, as you most likely know. A martyr is someone who "after [Christ's] example [has] proved the strength and genuineness of their faith in Christ by undergoing a violent death."

To testify before a judge. These are legal terms representing evidence cited in a judicial case (in this instance, the truth of salvation in Christ Jesus).

To give improper testimony is to perjure oneself, and thus be made a liar. So the concept of an unsaved person saying, "Well, that's okay for *you* to be a born-again Christian, because *you* believe that's true—but it's not really for me," is a cop-out and a slam against your character, because no matter what, that person is essentially saying, "You're a liar," because you've given false testimony. See the confrontation?

> *If we receive the witness of men, the witness of God is greater; for this is the witness of God which He has testified of His Son. He who believes in the Son of God has the witness in himself; he who does not believe God has made Him a liar, because he has not believed the testimony that God has given of His Son* (1 John 5:9-10).

Unsaved people make of God a liar. Bet you they don't think of it in those terms, but it's true. Would an atheist care? Probably not. But someone who believes in a Higher Power, and yet rejects the testimony of the Father through Jesus, calls God a liar.

Leaving aside this unsightly business of calling God a liar, the witness of God is greater than the witness of the world for His people, simply because it's based on eternal, spiritual principles. *He* knows His testimony is trustworthy. When He says something, will He not do what He says? (See Numbers 23:19.) So when we exercise our faith to see results, God will give His witness toward our actions, and we will see the accomplishment of that witness. He will testify of us as He testifies of the Son. Maybe our own witness is just to testify of our faith in Him, based on the earthly knowledge we have in what we've seen, or heard, or learned from His Word—but God's greater witness is sufficient to bear us up under any confrontation, in the natural or in the spiritual—even to the point of martyrdom!

Knowledge. That's another good word. In the Greek there's knowledge (*gnosis*, Strong's #1108, "know-sees"—1 Cor. 8:1 as an example); and then there's *knowledge* (*epignosis*, Strong's #1922, "eh-pig-no-sis"—Eph.1:17 as an example).

The first word is earthly knowledge, things we learn from contact with the natural world. It is where we get the word Gnostics. Or my favorite, agnostic (implying having no knowledge; ignorant…I'll let that settle for a second).

The second word bears the prefix *epi* which means "above or upon," among other things. So knowledge upon knowledge. Full knowledge, quite literally "above-knowledge." Thus, heavenly knowledge.

The Holy Spirit helps us by giving special revelation knowledge of the Father's heart-vision for humanity; but on a personal level, He gives us the necessary understanding of truth for our own unique purpose for being in the household of God.

One of these factors for evangelism is *revelation*. One of the Spirit's functions in this day and age is to impart within us a compelling drive to understand God's will for our lives.

We have to be made to understand the vision of the Father for winning the lost. This is our calling, above anything else He may have for us to do (see Eph. 1:15-19). The purpose of being called is so that we are released in those God-given abilities to ensure we are doing our utmost for those who are lost.

Revelation is another good Greek word: *apokalypsis* (Strong's #602, "ah-puh-call-up-sees") which you'll recognize Apocalypse—another name for the book of Revelation (clever, huh?). It means to take the lid off, to uncover, disclose, lighten, manifest, make appear. To unveil, reveal.

We can work with the Spirit in a number of ways to help this revelation component along. First, we need to see the needs of the people, to envision God's vision for our calling. Envision the vision. Not quite as cool as Apocalypse, but you get the point.

> *Put in the sickle, for the harvest is ripe.* **Come, go down;** *for the winepress is full, the vats overflow—for their wickedness is great* (Joel 3:13; we could say, Come, go down where the needs are).

Second, we must grasp hold of this vision. It's great for the Spirit to reveal to us the need, but if we don't act upon that revelation, nothing happens.

> *And from the days of John the Baptist until now the kingdom of heaven suffers violence, and the violent take it by force* (Matthew 11:12).

That phrase "suffers violence" is the same word as "pressing" in Luke 16:16: *"The law and the prophets were until John. Since that time the kingdom of God has been preached, and everyone is pressing into it."* The word implies application of force or "to be carried by a storm." It does mean to "inflict violence upon," but it is used almost entirely as a poetic, symbolic phrase.

The root of the word is *bios* (Strong's #979, "bee-oss") meaning, "life, living, what sustains or keeps something alive." It is the same prefix we use in biology, biography, or bioluminescence. To "be"-oss. If you'll pardon the play on words, *suffers violence* means, "to grab life by the *be-oss.*"

Forgive me…

In the poetic sense, we are to be violent. Taking life by force. Stepping up to help those needs of the people we have seen by the Spirit. Thayer's defines a violent person as one who "strives to obtain the kingdom's privileges with the utmost eagerness and effort." Basically, a person who feels a zealous, vehement desire to see the kingdom expanded. That is, grasping hold of the vision the Spirit has revealed to us.

Third, this revelation and this violence must be internalized for God's vision to be worthwhile. It is what we have experienced ourselves that we can interpret and bring to other people. *"But seek first the kingdom of God and His righteousness, and all these things shall be added to you"* (Matt. 6:33).

Last, what the Spirit has revealed of the vision of God, as we have seen those needs of the people, as we have grasped that vision by violence, we need to make ourselves available to execute that vision. We must become operative. But many of us have become *"dull of hearing"* (Heb. 5:11). The nonsense, or rather "veiled," teachings we have subjected ourselves to in many well-meaning, but ultimately lackadaisical, church settings have made many of us hesitant in being loosed by the Spirit.

But as we permit ourselves to be made to understand (to hear again), these events of the vision the Spirit reveals will simply blossom before our eyes, as we yield to the help of that same Spirit. This is why it is so important to implement the concepts discussed earlier in this book, to make way for the Intruder to help us "hear" once again.

This transfiguration into a violent, hearing, seeing, feeling saint—this renewing of our minds (see Rev. 12:1-2)—is cyclical. There are seasons when the Spirit presses upon us (violently) and fruit is grown, producing a harvest sometime in the future. That's no excuse to sit idle. There is *always* someone the Spirit is intruding upon. There is *always* some season upon us. We are challenged by our calling. No, we are *commanded* in it.

> *Go therefore and make disciples of all the nations, baptizing them in the name of the Father and of the Son and of the Holy Spirit, teaching them to observe all things that I have commanded you; and lo, I am with you always, even to the end of the age. Amen* (Matthew 28:19-20).

We are called to evangelize, but the thing is, to maximize that calling, in my opinion, requires a release of the miraculous, a manifestation of the truth, alongside the presented Word. We need to have an understanding of the anointing (see 1 John 2:20,27)—which requires the help of the Holy Spirit.

That anointing is the Holy Spirit Himself, yielding power.

> *How God anointed Jesus of Nazareth with the Holy Spirit and with power, who went about doing good and healing all who were oppressed by the devil, for God was with Him* (Acts 10:38).

A component of this kind of power (again, *dynamis*, Strong's #1411, "doo-na-miss;" that is, inherent power for miracles) is that it has the ability to reproduce itself, but only through constant use. Thus, if *dynamis* is not executed, it begins to wane away.

So joining the mandate for souls with the necessity *of dynamis* display, can we not see the importance of yielding to the aggressive workings of the Spirit in our lives?

MOTIVATION

Another factor of spreading the fame of Christ through miraculous evangelism is our *motivation*. After the Spirit has revealed, commanded and anointed, we need to determine *why* we do what we do.

Along with overwhelming power, the Spirit helps to produce grace in our lives. This is what John was saying: *"And of His fullness we have all received, and grace for grace. For the law was given through Moses, but grace and truth came through Jesus Christ"* (John 1:16-17). The fullness of Christ is the ability to be graced to receive grace.

Grace is unmerited favor. It is not cheap or easy, but it is something we don't deserve; yet is given freely, liberally, for the operational power to be expressed in truth. Grace, power, truth. Hand in hand. This is why we call the gifts listed in First Corinthians 12 "grace-gifts." You probably know the Greek word is *charis* (Strong's #5485, "k(h)ar-iss") where we get the word charismatic. It stems from a root meaning "to rejoice exceedingly, to be well, to thrive," and in fact is a word of greeting and salutation. It could be translated, "Hail! Fare thee well! Godspeed to you!"

> *But by the grace of God I am what I am, and His grace toward me was not in vain; but I labored more abundantly than they all, yet not I, but the grace of God which was with me* (1 Corinthians 15:10).

This grace is a motivating factor to share in His gifts for the benefit of another. *"Heal the sick, cleanse the lepers, raise the dead, cast out demons. Freely you have received, freely give"* (Matt. 10:8).

This is what Peter is admonishing us:

> *As each of you has received a gift (a particular spiritual talent, a gracious divine endowment), employ it for one another as [befits] good trustees of God's many-sided grace [faithful stewards of the extremely diverse powers and gifts granted to Christians by unmerited favor]. Whoever speaks, [let him do it as one who utters] oracles of God; whoever renders service, [let him do it] as with the strength which God furnishes abundantly, so that in all things God may be glorified through Jesus Christ (the Messiah). To Him be the glory and dominion forever and ever (through endless ages). Amen (so be it)* (1 Peter 4:10-11 AMP).

The Holy Spirit reveals our motivations, working in grace to fulfill the law of Christ, bearing one another's burdens—lifting others up (see Gal. 6:2-5).

But also He reveals our motivations in fulfilling the marked out course of God for our lives, in the name of evangelizing those around us, in whatever measure of ministry He has given us. *"...Take heed to the ministry which you have received in the Lord, that you may fulfill it"* (Col. 4:17).

We are told to "earnestly desire" these grace-gifts operating in our ministries (see 1 Cor. 12:31). It is not a sin to covet spiritual gifts if with the right motivation. That singular motivation is dual-natured: 1) to be for the edifying of the Church, and 2) for bringing in the lost. Any other type of motivation is idolatry and vain glory. But we are instructed to stir up and not neglect these grace gifts for the right reasons (see 1 Tim. 4:14-15; 2 Tim. 1:6,8).

But the more excellent way Paul speaks of in First Corinthians 13 is, of course, love!

Love is to be the primary motivation for evangelizing the lost and equipping the saints. Three purposes of ministry are: to comfort in love, to exhort in love, to edify in love. There's a lot of love in this paragraph. Can you feel it?

We are called to serve. To *cherish*. To make others warm (therapy, again). Through love we will see the greatest manifestation of the Son. We are told by Him to make ourselves servants and slaves—these are the greatest in the kingdom (see Matt. 20:25-28). The Bible makes it very clear that exhorting one another out of motivating love is *never* overlooked by God (see Matt. 10:42 as just one example).

And serving is not always a spiritual matter, but we are to serve in the natural, too. Philip and Stephen were of the seven appointed to the "mundane" aspects of running the church—even waiting on tables! (See Acts 6:2-4.) And yet, look how mightily they were used by God in signs, wonders, and miracles. While it might sound like a poor payoff to an unenlightened Christian, Stephen had the distinct place in all of history as the first martyr for Christ. Imagine his reward in heaven!

Being zealous for spiritual gifts, we are told to use them to edify the church, to comfort and edify one another, pursuing these things which make for peace (see 1 Cor. 14:12; 1 Thess. 5:11; Rom. 14:19). These should be our motivations for spreading the fame of Jesus Christ, and the Spirit will honor our true intentions!

RELEASE

A third factor is *release*. We know by now that we have a calling, a destiny, to spread the fame of Jesus, to manifest Him in a way rarely, if ever before, seen as sons of God. We need to be instructed by the Spirit on just how to release this anointing to the world at large. I find that a lot saints know *about* the anointing, but they may not know how to *release* that anointing for humankind's benefit. I shared a lot of information on the anointing in other works, but let's take a few moments and highlight some keys about being released in the anointing.

The Spirit has anointed us with gifts severally as He wills (see 1 Cor. 12:11). These gifts are to be used to release ourselves in the abilities of God, to act as He would in a particular situation or need, to do as He would do. But the anointing not only releases us, the dispensers of the gifts, but the recipients of the gifts as well. There is something required on their behalves, as well, in order for the fame of Christ to go forth.

There is also a need for a release from legalism into freedom. Not a popular subject, because it polarizes Christianity; but let's face it, there's a lot of legalism in the body of Christ. Has been for nearly 2,000 years. The release of the anointing combats this.

Stand fast therefore in the liberty by which Christ has made us free, and do not be entangled again with a yoke of bondage. Indeed I, Paul, say to you that if you become circumcised, Christ will profit you nothing. And I testify again to every man who becomes circumcised that he is a debtor to keep the whole law. You have become estranged from Christ, you who attempt to be justified by law; you have fallen from grace. For we through the Spirit eagerly wait for the hope of righteousness by faith (Galatians 5:1-5).

But on the other side of the token, I trust you're mature enough to know this release factor is not a free license to act like a fool. We need to grow up in the Lord, and just as Paul here was making bold in his statements concerning freedom versus legalism, I may take a little freedom myself in stating (in love) that this concept of doing whatever we want, acting however we want, upsetting whoever we want—all in the name of being "out from under the Law"—is about the height of spiritual ignorance and does away with about 90 percent of what the New Testament teaches.

Yes, I know the kingdom of heaven is neither food nor drink (see Rom. 14:17), but if you're getting soused every weekend, something's wrong. Neither is the kingdom of heaven "How much can I get away with?" Usually when you get to know the people who are so pro-grace with vehemence against anybody else trying to "stifle their freedom," there's a *reason* they need that kind of grace.

It's not just keeping our noses clean to be assured of salvation, but we don't want to become defiled Christians; and habitual sin unconfessed *will* cause defilement, no matter what you might've heard to the contrary. We need to keep a proper balance; teaching to any one extreme leads to error, and this isn't something we want to play around with.

Look, I'm not here to badger people. Let's just be careful, okay? All of us. You, me, and them. Let us all work out our salvation with much fear and trembling! (See Philippians 2:12.) There is *right* and there is *wrong*. It is not as gray as you might think. And freedom does not mean anything goes in the name of grace.

Yet legalism destroys Christian life. For let's be "fair and balanced":

> *This only I want to learn from you: Did you receive the Spirit by the works of the law, or by the hearing of faith? …Therefore He who supplies the Spirit to you and works miracles among you, does He do it by the works of the law, or by the hearing of faith?* (Galatians 3:2,5).

The answer should be rhetorical: the hearing of faith. Notice it's not (only) grace; it's the hearing of faith. Interesting to note that the word "supplies" here is the same Greek word as *"add* to your faith virtue" in First Peter 1:5. It is not (only) grace that supplies the Spirit, and virtue, and so on—it is the hearing of faith, sound doctrine and teaching. This is why the author of Hebrews says:

> *Therefore we must give the more earnest heed to the things we have heard, lest we drift away. For if the word spoken through angels proved steadfast, and every transgression and disobedience received a just reward, how shall we escape if we neglect so great a salvation, which at the first began to be spoken by the Lord, and was confirmed to us by those who heard Him, God also bearing witness both with signs and wonders, with various miracles, and gifts of the Holy Spirit, according to His own will?* (Hebrews 2:1-4)

It is the release of the Holy Spirit, once again, that glorious Intruder, working gifts out in your life according to His will—the release of the anointing—coupled with giving *"earnest heed to the things we have heard."* The Word and the Spirit, lest we drift away.

The works of the law (legalism) deaden the hearing of faith, stifling the aggressive work of the Spirit in our lives.

The release of the anointing is what breaks all bondages (see Isa. 10:27)—religious or otherwise. And it releases others, because many times, before people will embrace God directly, they will embrace what *we* represent. We are the pathway leading them to the Door.

The anointing is the manifest presence of God that can be felt through our five senses. This is what must be coupled with the hearing of faith—we must be released, working with the Holy Spirit, so that we are enabled to complete the activities God has directed in our lives.

"But the manifestation of the Spirit is given to each one for the profit of all" (1 Cor. 12:7). The purpose of releasing the anointing is to proclaim and to appoint (see Isa. 61:1-3, underline "proclaim" and "appoint" in that passage). The Spirit's work in our lives, through the anointing, is to create in us an ability "to do" (proclaim) and "to be" (appoint). To *look upward* to the Lord, so that we can *look inward* to ourselves, and then turn that *looking outward* to reach the people.

Isaiah looks upward and sees the Lord—he had a revelation of the Father's heart and His burden. Then he looks inward and sees his need for change ("I am undone!") and then after being anointed—and purified, for the anointing is tainted if we are not sanctified—by the live coal, he looks outward ("Here I am! Send me.") Here are three stages of "release" that apply most aptly to the demand of the Intruder on our lives to "be sent" to our areas of influence and initiate encounters with others to spread the fame of Jesus. (See Isa. 6:1,5,9).

That's what James was saying. Release. Answer the needs of those around us. Otherwise, what does the hearing of faith, the gifts of the Spirit, profit?

> *If a brother or sister is naked and destitute of daily food, and one of you says to them, "Depart in peace, be warmed and filled," but*

you do not give them the things which are needed for the body, what does it profit? Thus also faith by itself, if it does not have works, is dead (James 2:15-17).

The purpose of releasing the anointing is to minister to others (see Luke 4:18-19); and so that we might "see" (see Rev. 3:18) the things of the Lord; and so that we might "know" and discern (see 1 John 2:20,27).

"But he who endures to the end shall be saved" (Matt. 24:13). It's interesting to note that word "endures" means to tarry, to endure, to abide, to remain where one is at, to stand one's ground and not flee or turn backward. The release of the Spirit helps us to take a stand in the midst of persecution, to remain in one place and not back up, no matter what we may face.

The anointing is released so we might rule and reign (see 2 Sam. 5:3-4). We are anointed by the Spirit to receive from the Lord, just as Aaron was anointed and was given charge of the heave offerings (see Num. 18:8).

In short, the anointing is to be released, to release others. When Isaiah talks about the anointing breaking the yoke (again, see Isa. 10:27), the concept is the yoke—the weighing down of the enemy, infirmity, weakness—becomes so utterly destroyed, it is ground into bits, blown away by the wind. Theologians have said before, the connotation is one's spiritual neck becomes so fat by the anointing that the yoke will not go around. Sometimes it's good to be fat!

It takes the aggressive, overwhelming help of the Holy Spirit to become so fat and to release that "fatness" to others. We must be made to know that it is *"...not by **might** nor by **power**, but by My Spirit..."* (Zech. 4:6). That word "might" in the Hebrew speaks of an army, military strength in numbers, overwhelming the enemy by the strength of a team operation, sheer might. It is *not* by this means of mighty strength that we overcome. That word "power" means individual power, putting one's shoulder to the wheel, singlehandedly pushing past opposition. (Incidentally, the word also means a "lizard," some kind of small extinct, unclean reptile like a chameleon, but that's just free of charge.) At any rate, it is *not* by this means, individual power, that we overcome.

No, it is by the help of the Spirit, releasing His anointing, that we overcome, that we become "fat" and are able to help make others "fat."

We become vehicles to release God's revelation to others, for Christ's testimony is confirmed when we manifest His lordship into reality by the work of the Intruder. (See Revelation 19:10.) The Father's own testimony is confirmed by manifesting His greatness into reality. (See again Hebrews 2:4.) Those signs, wonders, and miracles each have a specific meaning.

"Signs" is a visible token of God's power—it is the *mark* or *imprint* of God on one's spirit, rendering a spiritual awakening that points toward the existence of God's power (not the chameleon kind).

"Wonders" speak of three specific ways God bears witness to people: an amazement (a wonder!), a sense of marveling (amazing!), and an admiration (wow!). Wonders appeal to the mind and intellect, compelling people to worship Him.

"Miracles" is the execution, or act, of exhibiting power that indicates the Source of the release. These appeal as much to the outward as to the inward, but touch all three attributes that make up a person: their spirit, soul, and body.

By operating in the release of the Spirit's anointing through signs, wonders, and miracles, the Church's testimony is confirmed when we manifest His reputation (His fame) into reality.

All of these release activities are for the express purpose of proving the testimony of Jesus, *"who being the brightness of His glory* [the Father's] *and the express image of His* [the Father's] *person, and upholding all things by the word of His power* [Jesus' power], *when He had by Himself purged our sins, sat down at the right hand of the Majesty on high*" (Heb. 1:3).

Truly Jesus manifested the reputation, or fame, of the Father into reality; and by the works of the Spirit, we manifest the reputation of our Lord:

> *Who also made us sufficient as ministers of the new covenant, not of the letter but of the Spirit; for the letter kills, but the Spirit gives life. ...how will the ministry of the Spirit not be more glorious? ...Now the Lord is the Spirit; and where the Spirit of the Lord is, there is liberty. But we all...are being transformed into the same image from glory to glory, just as by the Spirit of the Lord* (2 Corinthians 3:6,8,17-18).

This tells me we are to be ministers as Jesus was, being charged with the Spirit's power (anointing) to provide a *visible, audible, tangible* expression of God. As the Church is edified, thus it manifests His fame into reality. We must release the work of the Spirit within our lives!

Ultimately the anointing is a vehicle to release God's love. It's as simple as that. God *loves* people, and He wants them to come to Him, to worship Him, so that He might make them His own and spare them from an eternity apart from Himself.

RESULTS

The point of revelation, identifying our motivation and releasing the anointing, is to bring about *results*. Otherwise, what's the purpose? Really, getting results is a matter of *focus*. Being focused on releasing God's love, being focused on the Intruder, being focused on hearing God's voice in whatever particular situation we find ourselves in. It takes developing a sensitivity to *God's thoughts*, again an aggressive work of the Spirit.

This should be our petition of the Father:

So when they heard that, they raised their voice to God with one accord and said: "Lord, You are God, who made heaven and earth and the sea, and all that is in them...Now, Lord, look on their threats, and grant to Your servants that with all boldness they may speak Your word, by stretching out Your hand to heal, and that signs and wonders may be done through the name of Your holy Servant Jesus" (Acts 4:24,29-30).

I believe there is an element of incorporating the prophetic into our prayers as we allow the Spirit to help us discern God's thoughts. As we ask these things of God (healing, provision, boldness, comfort, protection, etc.), the Spirit gives prophetic instruction on how to go about executing God's thoughts to see the results we're asking for.

(Note: anything that Jesus provided in the atonement of the cross, we need not ask "God's will" in this matter. You don't need to get "God's mind" on *should* you be healed. The answer is Yes, God's will is *always* for His people to be healed. However, this prophetic instruction can help reveal *why* a healing has not taken place, or *how* a healing should take place. Not *if* a healing should take place; that was already settled at the cross.)

Focus to see results also takes developing a sensitivity to *God's words,* and thereby proclaiming what He would speak in any given situation. See Second Kings 6:18; Luke 13:11-13; and Acts 9:34. All of these scriptures are instances of proclaiming something, and it being executed by the Father, based on the *words of those praying.* That's awesome! It was according to the word of Elisha, his proclamation, that God blinded the Syrians. Jesus proclaimed the woman was loosed from her infirmity, and God made it so. It was Peter's proclamation to Aeneas that the Lord acted upon.

In fact, these acts of proclamation are really up to the proclaimer's faith, coupled with a gift of God's faith "downloaded" and activated for a specific need, and then God acts based on that mingled faith. See why the help of the Holy Spirit is so vital in seeing results?

Results come from focusing and developing a sensitivity to *God's authority*. These prayers of petition and proclamation turn into prayers of *command* as we gain an understanding of the Spirit's might through us.

> *Do you not believe that I am in the Father, and the Father in Me? The words that I speak to you I do not speak on My own authority; but the Father who dwells in Me does the works* (John 14:10).

Our Lord had perfect revelation concerning the Father's authority—He knew when to speak, when to be silent. He knew when to proclaim and when to command. We, too, by the help of the Spirit, should be striving for this sensitivity and understanding.

Look at the progression in Mark 7:32-35. Here the multitude brings a deaf and dumb (or impeded in speech) man before Jesus and *begs* Him to touch the man. (Petition based on God's thoughts.) Jesus takes the man aside from the multitude, puts His fingers in his ears and spits on his tongue. (This is the prophetic intuitiveness on *how* to act based on God's words.) Then, Jesus looks to heaven, sighs, and tells the ears and tongue to "be opened." (A command based on a revelation of God's authority.)

It's of some importance to point out, as in the case of Luke 4:38-39, when Jesus *commanded* ("rebuked the fever"), He was addressing the cause behind the attack, in this case a sudden spirit of illness. So He didn't petition the Father to remove the symptoms of the fever, but there was a prophetic intuition that revealed a spirit of infirmity to Jesus, which He promptly took authority over and rebuked. Again, it is imperative we allow the Spirit to develop this kind of sensitivity and intuition to know the reasons behind a hindrance or attack.

Not *everything* is a demon, I'll grant you, sometimes a fever is just a fever; but we deal with the demonic a lot more than people realize, and I think it's time we stopped kidding ourselves that the enemy doesn't try to oppress God's people. I'll share a little secret with you here that you may not like to hear: when I pray for people (born-again Christians) in services, about 90 percent of their healing comes from rebuking the demonic in their lives. That's not an exaggerated percentage. Nine times out of ten, a Christian's infirmity is rooted in a demonic harassment. So much so, that I think my next book is going to be on deliverance for the body of Christ. After all, it *is* the children's bread (see Matt. 15:21-28).

This sensitivity to God's authority over any weakness, be it demonic or otherwise, does not and cannot originate from our soulish realm, our "good intentions." It is not derived from *us* but rather *instilled* within us by the aggressive help of the Spirit. Our pity and sympathy isn't enough to activate these kinds of commands—it is solely an unction of God.

So one way to know that unction of God is to *sense* the accomplishment of what we're commanding *before* we actually see the results with human eyes. I'm talking about a release in the spirit realm here—not something we drum up or manufacture emotionally or mentally.

Think of it this way: this authority to command comes *through* us from God. We are simply empty vessels for the authority to flow through—we are not the creators of the authority.

And we should also remember that not every person we pray for is *ready* to receive a healing; there is training and preparation, the hearing of faith, on their part—and they must be in agreement with you in prayer. (Unless it is a sovereign act of God apart from your or their actions—which is mainly when someone is unsaved and the Lord is wooing them into the kingdom.) So again, developing a sensitivity to the work of the Spirit through you is important to be able to discern these things.

Ultimately, the greatest key to results is to be focused on *God's love*. Just as there is a law of power that gets people to look to the Lord for their healing, there is a higher law of love; operating in this law is what gets people in a place to receive that power. Just as John *continually* laid his head on Jesus' bosom (see John 13:23), we too must develop an abiding love relationship with our King and Bridegroom.

It takes more than just some casual encounter with the Lord to be changed. No matter what the Spirit does through you and with you, you cannot see the results in the magnitude that spreads the fame of Jesus Christ if you are not a lover. While it sounds contrary, it is a fact: the measure in which you are a lover of Jesus and of the people, is the measure to which you will be a warrior for Him. You're called to be a priest *and* a king (see Rev. 1:6). In their most boiled down state, results stem from giving out what we have received—and if we have not received love, we cannot give it out.

> *Now hope does not disappoint, because the love of God has been poured out in our hearts by the Holy Spirit who was given to us* (Romans 5:5).

I've said elsewhere we must learn to be sensitive to the unmet love needs of others. We must learn to walk in divine love, being guided and directed by it. Love must be manifested and projected on others to see the fame of Jesus spread. One cannot ask God for an increase of love, for it is a fruit of the Spirit, and only by His help can it be grown. We must learn to say, "Lord, with the measure of love that I have, let me give it out to others, so that the fruit of love might increase in my life." Remember, God has not told us to make love, peace, or joy *happen*—we must *bear* the fruit of the glorious Intruder, not make it.

I am the true vine, and My Father is the vinedresser. Every branch in Me that does not bear fruit He takes away; and every branch that bears fruit He prunes, that it may bear more fruit. ...I am the vine, you are the branches. He who abides in Me, and I in him, bears much fruit; for without Me you can do nothing. ...If you abide in Me, and My words abide in you, you will ask what you desire, and it shall be done for you. ...As the Father loved Me, I also have loved you; abide in My love. ...This is My commandment, that you love one another as I have loved you. Greater love has no one than this, than to lay down one's life for his friends (John 15:1-2,5,7,9,12-13).

To see results in love, we need to be focused on the following, in order:

1. See the needs of the people;

2. Take the first step toward meeting that need, don't wait for them to approach you;

3. Don't stop halfway, proceed and push for the manifestation as long as required;

4. Realize that the implanted urge (compassion) to minister to someone is from God;

5. The result and the incentive is then left up to God if you have been faithful in your pursuit of love (and He is faithful to perform!).

There is a law of power, a greater law of love, and a law of purpose. We must be focused on *God's purpose* for our lives. We must get people to stand for their rights and manifestation, to know they have a purpose and reason for being here.

For I know the thoughts that I think toward you, says the Lord, thoughts of peace and not of evil, to give you a future and a hope (Jeremiah 29:11).

In the original King James, future and hope is translated "expected end." The Hebrew for "expected" is literally a cord, something to bind and gather, a rope that brings something together, so poetically it is an expectancy for a future of great hope—to bind it all together. It is translated "the thing that I long for" in Job 6:8. A happy ending, prosperous, peaceful, riding into the sunset fulfilled. God has no delight in suffering (see Ezek. 18:23).

In Jeremiah 29:11, "For I know" could be paraphrased, "This is My intention. As a friend, I discern your need, and I have a full understanding of the answer to that need, so what has been fenced, I am letting loose!"

To see the results that spread the fame of the Lord, we must get the people to know they have a bright future; God cares for them and wants to see them reach their "expected end." So there is a law of perseverance, contending for the faith, to stand in our destinies because *"He who has begun a good work in you will complete it until the day of Jesus Christ"* (Phil. 1:6).

The Holy Spirit does not leave things unfinished. The glorious Intruder is pervasive and insistent. He won't let up in His help for your life, whether you are a child of God or still in the kingdom of darkness. He can't let up! The alternative is simply too horrible to bear.

Why must we press for results? Why must we evangelize? Why must we pursue the Spirit's work in our lives to translate that to others? Why must we pursue the lost with poetic violence? In the next chapter, let me share with you a revelation you might not like to know...

9

HOPELESS

In October 2012, I had a night vision. What I mean by this is I was asleep, but this was not a dream-state in my mind. I was not watching this in my mind's eye. I felt as if I were spiritually absent from my body (that it was left in bed, snoring) and my spirit-man was literally approached by an extremely bright angel. This was not the Lord Himself.

Now, I don't have encounters like these every time I catch some Zs, so please understand if I share this with you—it's a rare occurrence, and therefore, it's important. Maybe a dozen times in forty years has something like this happened.

This angel spoke to me audibly, and said, "The Lord wishes for me to show you the first level of the pit."

I won't argue with you if there are levels of hell or not. If your theology can't accommodate this, just accept that *I* believe this really happened to me, it was not some movie in my mind, and take it to the Spirit in prayer. As always, when I share an encounter such as this, I am extremely careful not to embellish any aspect of it. I know I will stand before God to give an account to just how accurate this night vision was. Therefore, you're going to have to take me at my word, and ask the glorious Intruder to bear witness with your spirit that I'm being truthful in what I'm about to recount.

As the angel spoke, we were instantly in hell.

The first thing that attacked me was the smell. It was an overpowering stench of sulfur and burning decay, like trash on fire, rotting refuse burning constantly. I knew we had gone straight down from my bed, through the ground and into the very belly of the earth. Yes, I am saying hell is on earth, a literal place like Arizona or Minnesota, in the center of this planet. It is not some ethereal state of mind, nor a metaphorical concept. It is a real place, and I was really there in spirit-form, not some misty ectoplasmic, floating apparition.

I cannot accurately describe the smell of hell. It seemed to seep into me, and is a form of judgment in itself. No one could ever get used to it, never become acclimated to it, it is always stifling and thick and almost tangible. This smell is the stench of unrepentant sin, it clings to the cavernous walls of hell, and it is this stench that offends the nostrils of the Lord.

I was aware of the sense of the need to breathe, the act of drawing this stench into my spirit-lungs, and I choked. I was nearly suffocating. It was difficult to breathe, and yet I felt that I must. I wanted to gag it out and found that I could not. It was so oppressive I thought it would smother me. (As a quick aside, even in a spiritual state, I possessed the same physical senses as here on earth: sight, hearing, touch, taste, and smell. I could think in my "brain" just like I can here on earth.)

I was upheld in the presence of this angel; otherwise, I would have been crushed by the smell of the place alone. This is what rebellion smells like to the Lord.

It was hotter than anywhere I have ever been on earth. The kind of heat that makes it so you cannot breathe. Like when you open the oven to pull out dinner, and a blast of heat takes your breath away, so you turn your head and gasp—but the heat follows you everywhere you turn.

After the heat and the smell assaulted me, and I mean that as literally as one can, I realized how absolutely dark it was. The angel himself glowed with exceedingly bright light, and from this glow I could make out black rock that was the walls of this plane. I was stunned by the sheer magnitude of the size of the place, yet I could see just faintly to the far end of this cavern because of the angel's radiating light. I also just knew in my spirit this was one section of hell, that there were many other such places, and we were viewing just one part of it. I got the sensation there were deeper pits beneath us, but I could not hear or see what was going on underneath us.

I believe had the angel not been there, it would've been in absolute darkness, not a speck of light at all, completely and totally, 100 percent dark. Imagine that. I have never known anything so utterly fearful as recognizing how *dark* hell is.

The next thing I became aware of was screaming. Not constant screaming. But every few seconds I would hear a moaning and a wailing from different places. It wasn't just the screaming of pain, as of someone being tortured (although there was this sound, too) but more often it was the howling, gut-wrenching sobs of someone in the throes of total despair and hopelessness.

The angel turned to me and said, "Hell is hopeless."

Just like that. And I understood, there was no refuge, there was no end of torment. It was eternal. I wish I could say that I believed the souls of the damned are eventually annihilated. That would be merciful, and in my human eyes, just; that they would've paid their penalty ultimately. But God *is* holy. And sin *will* be punished. Forever. It must take a very holy God to know that the millions and millions of souls in hell will never get amnesty. After just a few minutes in the place, I would've let them all off the hook, because I can't imagine, I can't even perceive in my mind, being there for eternity.

For even when the Lord takes hell and casts it into the lake of fire (see Rev. 20:14-15) and it is hurled from Him, these souls are still existing in torment. I personally believe this is why the cosmos is never-ending, the lake of fire will go out farther from the presence of God for all time infinity.

That was the most horrific revelation. There was no presence of God felt anywhere. None. To know one was completely cut off and isolated from the Creator was to wish one could go insane, and one could not. Even with the angel by my side, I felt something encroaching on my mind that I would lose it in a moment, and there would almost be a kind of relief in going crazy, but I could not. I had to stand there and take it all in, just as it is.

We sometimes forget to realize, that even if we can't sense it, the presence of God is on this earth all the time. Down there, He had removed His presence wholly, and the people groaned in torment. I could literally hear them gnashing their teeth as they moaned.

We must understand that God did not create hell for humanity. It was designed for the devil and his fallen angels and demons. It is humankind's choice to go to hell by rejecting salvation in Jesus Christ.

Here's something I have difficulty explaining. There were flames around us. But they cast *no light,* they were completely black flames that I would've been unable to see, except for the glow of the angel falling on them. These flames flickered like flames here on the surface, but there was no red or orange or white or blue, no reflection of light whatsoever. They were perfectly black flames; it's the only way I can describe it.

Farther at our feet were these black kind of shrub-like "plants"—scrubby and skeletal, maybe a bit like coral in the ocean. I was amazed there was some kind of vegetation down here, for in the natural nothing could possibly grow.

The bleakness of the landscape around us was just like a cave. And in the center of this cave was a large black pool. I mean, I could barely discern its banks at the opposite end, so it did not go on for-ever—it was a real lake, but it was not filled with water. Somehow in my spirit I knew there were many, many of these kinds of lakes, perhaps thousands, all throughout the belly of the earth. This was the first level of hell, the angel told me.

He told me I was unprepared for the lower levels and this was all he was instructed to show me. That my own spirit would not be able to uphold me in this place, were it not for the protection of the Lord that surrounded him and me, and that even though I could not sense His presence, I was only kept from the horrors by His sustaining grace. Indeed, Christ has the keys to hell, and even it must obey Him. But if I was being *kept* from the horrors, feeling as I did, I didn't even want to know what the inhabitants were suffer-ing. Our minds cannot comprehend the terrors of hell; it is beyond adequate human description.

The chaos of hell is inexpressible: the wailing every few seconds, the stench and the heat, the darkness and the hopelessness. It is like a constant state of upheaval, turmoil, and panic. I felt if I could just have one or two moments of peace to collect my thoughts, I would be able to withstand this attack on my senses, but there was no reprieve. It was constant—threatening to envelop me on all sides. Disorder reigned and even the landscape seemed unstable; it appeared to change in the light cast by the angel. Chaos.

Chained to the walls of this cavern were huge demons. They were chained so that they could not completely bowl over the spirits, such was their vehemence against the damned. If it would've been possible to consume a spirit being, they would've tried, had their chains not kept them just out of reach.

The only way I can describe these demons is to say they were very large and similar to those big trolls in one of the *Lord of the Rings* movies. Because of the dimness, I could not tell their color, if they had hair, or specific details about their faces. Other than they were snarling and foul. Their arms were longer than their torsos and they jerked on their chains, spitting, roaring in anger that they could not completely destroy the spirits in hell. These guttural sounds were panic-inspiring, as was the clanking of these huge chains that kept them just out of reach of the lake.

They spoke a horrible, grunting, howling language, but I understood that they were mocking the damned, taunting them, threatening them with what they would do if they were to break free of these chains.

What filled the crater lake was a thick black viscous substance, like oil but more foul-smelling, rancid in decay. It was not completely opaque. In the light of the angel's presence, I was able to discern that within the large crater there were dozens and dozens, maybe even hundreds of smaller cavities or pits *underneath* this black goo. And within each pit was a spirit-body in torment. Under this "water."

I gasped in panic. There were *people* under the black water, crammed into these shallow holes, forced to breathe in this slimy substance!

Each pit under the sludge was isolated. Normally, these tortured souls would be in total seclusion from anyone else for all eternity.

We were now near the crater's edge, looking down into the nearest few pits. I saw the people writhing under the oily water. The angel said, "The blackness is their sin. They are forced continually to inhale the substance and it courses through them, reminding them why they are here, what kept them from the salvation and love of God. As they ingest the sin anew, they can never break free from its torment. For all eternity they remember why they have been condemned. The remembrance itself is judgment, for they wish they could forget." He repeated, "Hell is hopeless."

Four or five spirits were permitted to rise out of the nearest pits, and I stumbled back. How can I describe them to you? They were like desiccated corpses. Not entirely skeletons, for clumps of tattered flesh hung from their bones, as if they had been ripped apart by the black sludge or the demons, and the thought came to me that this was correct on both accounts. What I mean to say here is that their spirit-bodies *are* tortured in hell, and yet they cannot die. Their faces were skulls; however, there were sunken eyes within the sockets, full of misery and terror. I could recognize they were human, male and female, and the look of their eyes was the most unnerving sight I'd yet seen.

As they rose out of the water, they began to moan and shriek like the other voices I heard throughout the cavern. Not so much from physical pain (although they did look to be in agony) but from the torment within them—knowing the black oil coursing through them was their own sins and rebellion.

In Mark 9, where Jesus speaks about "their worm does not die," (verses 44, 46, 48, quoting Isa. 66:24), I believe it goes beyond just the metaphor of the always-burning Gehenna fires where worms (the Greek word is "maggot, grub") devoured the corpses of those who didn't fall into the flames. This sludge of sin remembrance coursed through these spirit-bodies eternally, eating away at the rotted flesh, as maggots do. That is why it is "their" worm, *their* sin, and it doesn't ever die.

It's difficult to describe, as most of this is, but "their worm does not die" showed me their spirit-bodies would "morph," for lack of a better term; the black liquid that clung to their tattered forms actually changed them into grotesque configurations.

The sin mutated them, like it mutated or warped the surroundings of the cavern. They appeared "unstable," shifting into horrid forms as the black water covered them. Even when they came out of the water, it clung to them. It was their sin and rebellion that was producing these repulsive, contorting mutations. I had a realization that this is the same effect that warped the demons and fallen angels, turning them into what they are now.

When these spirit-bodies stood in the black lake, the demons chained to the walls lunged for them, growling and cursing. I saw one spirit, who had once been female, approach the land's edge where the angel and I were standing. A look of relief came into those haunted eyes, not because of the angel or myself, but because the spirit had seen the gnarled black shrub near our feet. Without the angel's light, I don't think normally we would've been able to see the plant-thing, but I could be wrong.

"Moisture," the spirit whimpered. "If I could just have a drop of moisture. Just something to wet my lips. One drop to help this heat."

I could actually feel the elation and anticipation, the *hope* that even a split-second's relief one drop of moisture would bring her.

As her bone-like spirit-fingers curled around the plant, eyes so emotionally charged at the thought of one drop of water, how it would make this hell a tiny bit more bearable, even if just for a moment, if only this plant would give her one drop of moisture, please, God, have mercy... (Lord, I wanted her to have one drop!) Please, one drop, that's all...

The plant shattered into pieces in her hands and crumbled into dust.

A moan, a cry unlike anything I've ever heard in my whole life, so horrific, so wailing that I thought I would burst, so full of anguish at the cruelness of this latest torment, rent the foul, stifling air. She flailed and her eyes took on a maddened look, but she could not go insane, she could not forget. The demons chortled and mocked in laughter, clanking their chains, as the spirit howled in frustration and torment. She gnashed her teeth, snarling, like a dog being tormented with a stick.

"Hell is hopeless," the angel said.

The demon closest to us roared something in its weird speech and banged its chain on the stone. The spirits cowered, and I understood exactly what it had said, "Get back in the pits!"

They all began to shuffle into the black tar-water, moaning in agony as the stuff coursed up their ragged spirit-bodies and into their mouths, down and through, up again, forever. One by one, to the jeers of the demons, they began to sink back into their smaller holes, under the surface. The last to go was the woman who held the plant. Her plagued eyes met mine, and I sank to my knees.

"How?" I asked her, struggling for every breath. "How can you *handle* this?"

The sadness and the anger, the torment and the pain, the rage and the madness, the fear and the belligerence in her eyes was something I'll never, ever forget. It was the worst thing I'd seen so far—that look.

She spoke to me, and I quote her verbatim:

"Well," she said. "At *least* I'm not down *there*." And she pointed lower into hell, then slipped beneath the oily surface.

EPILOGUE

THE ANGEL GRABBED ME AND TOOK ME UP. I AWOKE IN MY BED, stifling a scream. I was trembling from head to toe, soaked in sweat, the grime and dirt, the stench, the panic and fear. I had to shower, but I was shaking so much that I couldn't crawl out of bed. I'm not sure if I can handle *these* kinds of rapture or translation experiences. If this was only the first level, please God, don't show me the next.

I know that's a pretty heavy way to end a book, but we need to be made to understand how vital it is, this aggressive, overwhelming intrusion of the Holy Spirit in our lives, working with us and through us to spread the fame of Jesus Christ by signs, wonders, and miracles. The whole point of this process, this book even, is not just "How cool is that to be used by the Spirit?" or "How awesome would it be to manifest the supernatural works of Jesus Christ?"

The reason behind this process is we are in a race against the clock. People are dying and going to hell. We as born-again Christians believe this with every fiber of our being—that we're right: there is a hell, and those who reject the Lord are rejected by the Father. Thus, the Spirit is racing, rushing, pushing, pulling, *intruding* in every way imaginable to spare people this fate. The world *must* have a reality check through the supernatural, showing there are only two paths they can go, one leads up, the other leads down.

And when He [the Spirit] *has come, He will convict the world of sin, and of righteousness, and of judgment* (John 16:8).

That is the Spirit's purpose here, to convict those still lost that there is such a thing as sin, and all are guilty of it, everyone on the planet. But it's not hopeless, for there is righteousness found in Jesus Christ. There is judgment because sin will be judged, and those found without the Lord's righteousness will be judged along with it.

This is why the Spirit is aggressive, so pursuing, because He knows *exactly* what's under the black water in hell. Salvation of souls, it's a simple concept, and it's what really matters to God. Not that the walk of the Spirit in our lives *after* we come to salvation is unimportant. But without that first saving grace, we're doomed the moment we're born.

(Well, rather, once we have an understanding of our fallen nature and the plan of salvation through Jesus Christ, at any rate—while we are all born with a sin nature that is spiritually deadened toward God, the age of accountability toward acceptance or rejection of His salvation may not be the same for all people. And I did *not* see any children in hell; they were all adults.)

Look, it's not difficult to understand what a Christian believes. The Holy Spirit must make it *real* to the people out there in the world; so if He has to intrude upon my life and bring me out of my comfort zone, work through me, change me, overpower my weaknesses, then so be it! Come, Holy Spirit, I say, come!

You should say this too!

SALVATION

No matter what you may have heard, salvation is not difficult to receive; it is a free gift received by believing in your heart and speaking with your mouth that you trust in Jesus Christ *alone* for salvation. There is *no other way.* If you want that assurance, pray this prayer to God and mean what you say. If you do, you will be saved. It really is that simple.

God, I believe You are real. I believe that I am a sinner, and that without Your grace and forgiveness, I am destined to go to hell when I die. But I believe Your Word when You say that You don't want anyone to perish, and that You gave Your only begotten Son, Jesus Christ, who is even God Himself, to die for my sins and pay the penalty for my rebellion against You. I believe in my heart You raised Him from the dead after three days, and that He is now seated with You in heaven. I confess with my mouth that I want Jesus to be Lord of my life. Forgive me of my sins; I turn away and repent from a lifestyle that is against Your ways. Lord Jesus, come into my heart and make me a new creation that will always desire to do Your will, to be holy as You are holy. Make me a new person and live inside me. I thank You that by faith, I believe I am now born again by Your Spirit, and I will serve You the rest of my days.